TRACKING TORTOISES

THE MISSION TO SAVE A
GALÁPAGOS GIANT

KATE MESSNER

WITH PHOTOGRAPHS BY JAKE MESSNER

For the ever-curious Matthew and Oliver

For more digital content, download a QR code reader app on your tablet or other smart device. Then scan the QR codes throughout the book to see tortoises and scientists in action!

Millbrook Press™
An imprint of Lerner Publishing Group, Inc.
241 First Avenue North
Minneapolis, MN 55401 USA

For reading levels and more information, look up this title at www.lernerbooks.com.

Image credits: All images provided by Jake Messner and Kate Messner, with the exception of: Ian Kennedy/Shutterstock.com, p. 3; © CDF, pp. 8 (right), 43 (bottom right); © Joshua Blake, CDF, pp. 9 (top left), 46, 47, 48 (left); © Juan Manuel Garcia, CDF, pp. 9 (top right), 43 (center right); LKW/Independent Picture Service, pp. 11 (both), 12 (left), 20 (both), 38, 50; Vladislav T. Jirousek/Shutterstock.com, pp. 13 (right), 22 (bottom); © Leonard Darwin, p. 14 (top right); Smith Archive/Alamy Stock Photo, p. 15 (left); © Carlton Ward Jr., p. 16 (left); SL-Photography/Shutterstock.com, p. 22 (top); © Sam Rowley, p. 29 (bottom); Wolfgang Kaehler/LightRocket/Getty Images, p. 33 (right); © Max Panck Institute/MoveBank, p. 36 (all maps); © Stephen Blake, pp. 36 (all tortoise photos), 56 (right); NOTE OMG/Shutterstock.com, p. 43 (bottom left); © Joshua Vela Fonseca/FCD, p. 48 (right). Design element: Gordana Simic/Shutterstock.com. Front cover: © Joshua Vela Fonseca/FCD; Girish HC/Shutterstock.com. Back cover: © Jake Messner. Jacket flaps: © Jake Messner; Girish HC/Shutterstock.com.

Designed by Kimberly Morales.
Main body text set in Metro Office. Typeface provided by Linotype AG.

Library of Congress Cataloging-in-Publication Data

Names: Messner, Kate, author.
Title: Tracking tortoises : the mission to save a Galápagos giant / Kate Messner.
Description: Minneapolis : Millbrook Press, [2022] | Includes bibliographical references and index. | Audience: Ages 9–14 | Audience: Grades 4–6 | Summary: "Take a journey to the Galápagos Islands to see Galápagos giant tortoises up close and discover how cutting-edge technology is helping scientists study and protect these gentle giants. Page Plus links in the book lead to videos of scientists in the field"— Provided by publisher.
Identifiers: LCCN 2020053050 (print) | LCCN 2020053051 (ebook) | ISBN 9781541596115 (library binding) | ISBN 9781728419039 (ebook)
Subjects: LCSH: Galapagos tortoise—Conservation—Galapagos Islands. | Galapagos Islands.
Classification: LCC QL666.C584 .M47 2022 (print) | LCC QL666.C584 (ebook) | DDC 597.92/46—dc23

LC record available at https://lccn.loc.gov/2020053050
LC ebook record available at https://lccn.loc.gov/2020053051

Manufactured in the United States of America
1-47627-48108-2/24/2021

CONTENTS

INTRODUCTION 4

CHAPTER 1
AN ARCHIPELAGO HOME 10

CHAPTER 2
STRUGGLE FOR SURVIVAL 18

CHAPTER 3
BABY GIANTS 26

CHAPTER 4
TRACKING HERBERT 34

CHAPTER 5
A NEW TORTOISE FOR THE TEAM 40

CHAPTER 6
FROM VOLCANO TO LABORATORY 46

CHAPTER 7
TOMORROW'S TORTOISES 52

A GALÁPAGOS TORTOISE TIMELINE 60

GLOSSARY 61

SOURCE NOTES 61

BIBLIOGRAPHY 62

FURTHER READING 63

INDEX 64

Try to keep up with Freddy!" researcher Stephen Blake calls from behind as we hike along a rugged trail toward the sandy lowlands where Galápagos giant tortoises nest.

But Freddy Cabrera is already half a football field ahead of us, bounding over wobbly, sharp volcanic rocks in his yellow rubber boots. He's been traveling this rocky, muddy path ever since he was a kid growing up in the Santa Cruz highlands, hunting goats with his father. Now Freddy makes the trek as a boots-on-the-ground researcher for the Galápagos Tortoise Movement Ecology Programme.

Today, we're out tracking tortoises.

I'm a hiker at heart. I've scaled more than thirty of the forty-six Adirondack High Peaks in New York State. But hiking on the island of Santa Cruz is different. The mud is red and slippery. Volcanic rocks wobble and tumble over one another with every step. Back home, I'd reach for a nearby tree to steady myself, but here, nearly everything is prickly. One wrong hand placement leads to a palm full of opuntia cactus thorns. One step off the trail and the perfectly named cat's claw plant rakes any bare skin like a rambunctious kitten.

By the time we reach the lowlands, where the tortoises nest, I'm tired, sweaty, and bleeding a little. I've also acquired a whole new respect for giant tortoises. The trail we've been hiking is the tortoises' migration route. They walk it on fat, stubby legs each year, carrying 50-pound (23 kg) shells the whole way.

It's not easy being a giant tortoise. That's part of the reason Cabrera and Blake are so invested in this project. What creature would choose to make such an exhausting

Tortoises rest on a trail in the Santa Cruz highlands.

migration year after year? Scientists believe the journey must be essential to the tortoises' survival. So what might happen to these endangered giants if their migration were no longer possible?

"Oh!" Blake calls out and points into the brush. He's spotted our first tracked tortoise of the morning, a five-year-old male with a radio transmitter glued to his shell. That transmitter sends out silent radio waves that allow scientists to pinpoint the tortoise's location. Otherwise, finding their research subjects in this rocky wilderness would be next to impossible.

The scientists greet their old friend by name—Angel (pronounced ahng-hel). All the tortoises are given names when they're tagged. Blake says that's better than assigning them numbers. "If Angel were AKBS7," he explains, "we might not remember what he was like the day we tagged him, when he was just this tiny little tortoise." Over the past ten years, Blake and his team have tagged and named more than 140 tortoises.

"Estás muy grande, Angel!" Blake gushes about how big the soccer-ball-sized tortoise has grown since he last

Researchers spot Angel, one of their tagged tortoises, among the volcanic rocks.

saw him a couple of years ago, as if Angel is a young nephew he hasn't visited in a while. These researchers feel great affection for their subjects. They're rooting for the hatchlings to survive—and to make it to the age of maturity in their twenties. That's when they'll likely begin to migrate, like many of the adult tortoises. But their future isn't guaranteed.

These tortoises live in one of the most unique places on Earth. Located more than 600 miles (966 km) off the coast of Ecuador, the Galápagos Islands have been a remote, unspoiled sanctuary for plants and animals that don't live anywhere else in the world. They're home to birds with feet as blue as the sky and prehistoric-looking iguanas that swim in the sea. But these islands, isolated from the rest of the world for so long, are changing. More people live there now, and many more come to visit each year. There are more buildings and more farms, and that means less open, wild land for tortoises to roam. Invasive species have poured into the islands too, and the ocean is warmer than it used to be.

What will these changes mean for Angel and the other endangered tortoises? Will they survive to maturity, when tortoises begin to migrate? And if they do, will that migration still be possible? That's what this team of rock-hopping researchers is hoping to find out.

Blue-footed boobies nest on land at night but spend much of their day flying over the ocean, hunting for fish.

MEET THE TORTOISE SCIENTISTS

STEPHEN BLAKE

Title: Coordinator of the Galápagos Tortoise Movement Ecology Programme

Education: Bachelor of Science in Zoology from University of London, Masters of Science in Resource Management, and PhD in Ecology from University of Edinburgh

As a student, Steve wasn't sure what career he wanted. "Except that I didn't fancy doing a normal job," he says. So he worked at a stable and as a zookeeper. Then he got a job working with gorillas and, later, elephants in the Congo Basin of Africa. Steve turned his attention to tortoises after his wife, wildlife veterinarian Sharon Deem, took a job in the Galápagos Islands. That was back in 2007, and he's been tracking tortoises ever since.

FREDDY CABRERA

Title: Field researcher with the Charles Darwin Foundation

Education: Studied biology in high school on Santa Cruz

Freddy grew up on a farm in the Santa Cruz highlands and spent his free time hiking through the forest, hunting feral goats and pigs with his father. When he graduated from school, he went to work hunting goats as part of a project to eradicate, or get rid of them, on islands where they'd been introduced. The goats were threatening giant tortoises by competing with them for food. After that job was complete, Cabrera started working for the Galápagos Tortoise Movement Ecology Programme. Thanks to all the time he spent outdoors growing up, he knows the territory of the tortoises better than anyone.

SHARON L. DEEM

Title: Director of the Saint Louis Zoo Institute for Conservation Medicine

Education: Doctorate of Veterinary Medicine from the VA/MD College of Veterinary Medicine and Zoo and Wildlife Residency and PhD in Veterinary Epidemiology from the University of Florida, Diplomate of the American College of Zoological Medicine

Sharon Deem grew up near the National Zoo in Washington, DC. She used to skateboard through the zoo looking at the pandas and other animals. At home, her bed was full of stuffed animals, most with Band-Aids. Sharon always wanted to be a veterinarian, and her work has taken her all over the world. She met Steve in Africa when she was the wildlife veterinarian in charge of immobilizing the elephants he was studying.

AINOA NIETO CLAUDIN

Title: Researcher for the Charles Darwin Foundation and Saint Louis Zoo Institute for Conservation Medicine

Education: Veterinary Medicine degree from the Complutense University of Madrid and currently working on a PhD in Veterinary Medicine

Ainoa Nieto Claudin grew up in Madrid, Spain, and has wanted to be a veterinarian since she was four years old. Her aunt was a vet, and by the time she was ten, she was helping out at her aunt's clinic, even assisting with surgeries. She says working with the Galápagos Tortoise Movement Ecology Programme in the Galápagos Islands is a dream come true.

IRENE PEÑA

Title: Volunteer with the Charles Darwin Foundation

Education: Veterinary Medicine degree from the Complutense University of Madrid

Irene grew up in a family with lots of animals— everything from dogs and cats to cows and pigs. She was interested in medicine but wasn't sure she wanted to work with people, so her mom suggested veterinary medicine. She volunteered with the foundation for a year, helping to prepare samples for analysis in the lab.

CHAPTER 1

AN ARCHIPELAGO HOME

It's impossible to understand Galápagos giant tortoises without exploring the archipelago, or series of islands, they call home. How did these islands form, and why is this ecosystem so special? How has evolution shaped the animals that live here? And what role do giant tortoises play in the story of the Galápagos?

These volcanic islands began rising out of the sea millions of years ago, thanks to a hot spot in the Pacific Ocean. A hot spot is a place where Earth's mantle—the molten layer beneath the crust—is hotter than usual. In those hot spots, magma pushes up through the crust to form volcanoes. And when this happens in the sea, those volcanoes can grow into islands. This is how island chains such as the Galápagos and Hawaiian Islands are formed.

But why are there multiple islands if there's just one hot spot? Because Earth's crust isn't just one big piece of rock. It's made of large plates that are constantly moving. The Galápagos Islands are close to where two plates meet—the Cocos Plate and the Nazca Plate.

The Galápagos Islands are on the Nazca Plate. As that plate moves, the hot spot beneath it stays put. Imagine holding a lit candle and passing a big sheet of plywood over it.

Different parts of the wood would burn as you moved it over the candle. That's sort of what happens with hot spots and Earth's plates. The hot spot pushes up magma in different locations as the plate moves above it. Because of this, the easternmost islands in the archipelago, San Cristóbal and Española, were formed first. But eventually, the Nazca Plate carried those islands away from the hot spot, so those

The Galápagos Islands are located close to where the Cocos and Nazca Plates meet.

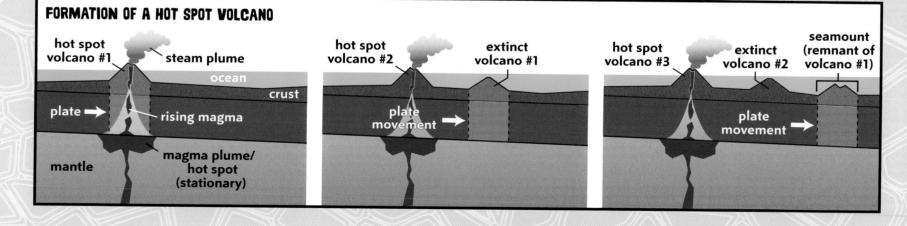

FORMATION OF A HOT SPOT VOLCANO

hot spot volcano #1
steam plume
ocean
crust
plate →
rising magma
mantle
magma plume/ hot spot (stationary)

hot spot volcano #2
extinct volcano #1
plate movement →

hot spot volcano #3
extinct volcano #2
seamount (remnant of volcano #1)
plate movement →

islands stopped growing, and new islands began to form. Western islands, such as Fernandina and Isabela, are newer and have regular volcanic activity. Some of the westernmost islands are still being formed today.

How do plants and animals come to live on volcanic islands that grow out of the sea? Because birds can fly, they're often the first to arrive. Other animals make a long, long journey by sea.

Scientists believe the first giant tortoises floated to the Galápagos Islands from the South American mainland millions of years ago, after a flood washed them out to sea.

Other reptiles such as iguanas and lizards likely arrived the same way, drifting on trees or clumps of vegetation. Because reptiles are cold-blooded, they can go longer than mammals without food and water, so they were able to survive that long ocean voyage. Scientists think sea lions and flightless birds also made their way to the Galápagos after being swept up in storms that took them far from home. Some plants probably arrived this way as well. Others were hitchhikers, sprouting from seeds that flew over the ocean in the digestive tracts of far wandering seabirds.

However they arrived, the plants and animals that first inhabited the Galápagos Islands were only the beginning of the remarkable story of life on this archipelago. Over the years, these species multiplied—and changed so much that they gave rise to brand-new species that now live only in Galápagos. We call these one-place-on-earth animals endemic species. One of them is the marine iguana, which looks like a regular land iguana but spends much of its day

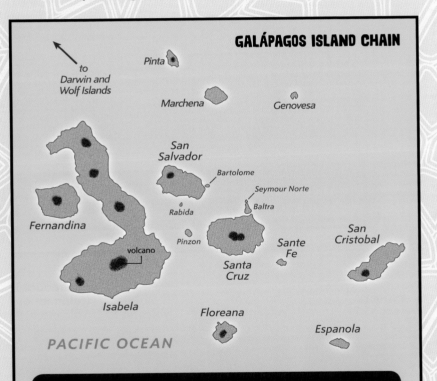

GALÁPAGOS ISLAND CHAIN

to Darwin and Wolf Islands

Pinta

Marchena

Genovesa

San Salvador

Bartolome

Seymour Norte

Rabida

Baltra

Fernandina

Pinzon

Sante Fe

San Cristobal

volcano

Santa Cruz

Isabela

Floreana

Espanola

PACIFIC OCEAN

The Galápagos archipelago consists of thirteen main islands along with many smaller islands, islets, and rocks that stick up from the sea. Each of the main islands came from a single volcano except Isabela, which was formed when six volcanoes joined together above sea level.

Marine iguanas have long, sharp claws that help them hold onto slippery rocks, both onshore and underwater.

foraging for algae growing on rocks in the sea. Marine iguanas crawl and sprawl all over one another on Galápagos shorelines, diving into the surf when it's time to eat. Scientists believe these unique iguanas evolved from the land iguanas that came from South America.

How does that happen? In a rugged place like the Galápagos Islands, animals have to compete for resources. Somewhere along the way, some land iguanas ventured into the sea looking for food. Because of the natural variations that happen in organisms, every once in a while, an iguana would show up with longer claws for gripping wet rocks, a flatter tail for swimming and diving, or a square face that made it easier to eat algae off rocks. Those iguanas had an advantage, so they got plenty of food. They did well and reproduced and passed on those helpful traits to their offspring. We call this process natural selection.

A marine iguana uses its sharp teeth to eat algae off shoreline rocks.

HOW EVOLUTION WORKS

Traits are characteristics that can be passed down from one generation to the next. They're passed along from parent to offspring and can include everything from the shape of a tortoise's shell to the size of a plant's leaves to the color of a person's eyes. Traits are encoded in a special molecule called deoxyribonucleic acid (DNA), which includes instructions for the development, functioning, and growth of an organism. There's a lot of variation in how traits are expressed, which means that organisms of the same species don't always end up looking the same. And sometimes mutations, or changes, in an organism's DNA lead to even bigger variations.

When a mutation is beneficial to an organism, that animal is more likely to survive and pass the trait down to its offspring. Over time, there will be more and more organisms with that helpful trait. This is natural selection—the process by which organisms that are best suited to their environment are more likely to survive, reproduce, and make more organisms that look like them. These variations in traits are important because some help the organism, and some don't.

This is why species change over time and why sometimes they change so much that brand-new species emerge. We call this process evolution.

The shape of a giant tortoise's shell can help it survive by making it easier for the tortoise to reach food.

Eventually, those seagoing iguanas were only mating with other iguanas with those same traits. That led to a whole new species of iguana, different from those that had stuck to eating cacti and other plants on land. This is how new species appear in the world, and it's happened quite a bit in the Galápagos Islands. It's made the islands a hot spot for scientists who study evolution—how species change over time through the process of natural selection.

In the Galápagos Islands, there are many different species of giant tortoises, iguanas, and finches. But scientists believe all of those animals evolved from common ancestors. The tortoises and iguanas that floated away from their mainland homes millions of years ago evolved into different species with different traits. And those first finches that flew to the islands, after multiplying and changing over time, gave rise to the many species of finches that live there today.

A naturalist named Charles Darwin shared some of the first ideas about natural selection and evolution. He wrote a book called *On the Origin of Species* after he visited the islands for five weeks in 1835. Darwin had noticed how the mockingbirds and tortoises on different islands had different traits that seemed to be specially tailored to where they lived. When he got home, he did more thinking about what he'd observed and eventually came to the conclusion that new species come about because of natural selection. This idea was incredibly controversial at the time. It conflicted with what some people's religion had taught them about God creating all the animals in just days. But by studying fossils and observing living animals, other scientists were able to prove that organisms evolve, or change, over time, and that's how new species come to be.

Charles Darwin's book *On the Origin of Species* was first published in 1859.

A land iguana feasts on a cactus pad.

A Galápagos mockingbird perches on a branch.

The unique animals of the Galápagos each play a role in the islands' terrestrial, coastal, and marine ecosystems. Marine iguanas climb over the rugged shorelines, blending into the black rocks as if they're made of lava themselves. Just up from the shoreline, their distant cousins, the land iguanas, rest in the sun and feast on cactus pads while smaller lava lizards dart over the rocks. These plant-eating reptiles play an important role in seed dispersal. The seeds that pass through their digestive systems sprout so that new plants can grow, providing food for other animals.

The Galápagos Islands are also home to more than sixty species of birds, many of which also help the islands' plants. Some are pollinators as well as seed spreaders. Mockingbirds serve this dual role. So do some of the finches that seem ever-present in the islands, flitting from branch to branch, perching on cacti, and pecking at the ground for seeds. Darwin collected some of those finches during his 1835 visit and wondered why their beaks came in so many shapes and sizes. It was one of the sparks for his ideas about evolution.

Darwin's finches are endemic species, as are most of the land birds in the islands. But only a handful of shorebirds are found only in the Galápagos: the Galápagos penguin, flightless cormorant, Galápagos petrel, waved albatross, swallow-tailed gull, and lava gull.

Other Galápagos shorebirds are native to the islands but can also be found elsewhere. These include the blue-footed boobies and frigate birds that nest in bushes near the rocky shores. Fluffy white chicks wait for their feathers to fill in while their parents soar overhead and dive-bomb into the waves to catch fish.

These birds, too, play an essential role in the Galápagos web of life by transferring nutrients between the marine and terrestrial ecosystems. When the birds feed on marine life and then return to their nesting sites, their guano, or poop, adds phosphorous and nitrogen to the soil, which helps coastal plants grow.

"Seeing this gradation and diversity of structure in one small, intimately related group of birds, one might really fancy that from an original paucity of birds in this archipelago, one species had been taken and modified for different ends."
—Charles Darwin, *The Voyage of the Beagle*

Above: A blue-footed booby chick calls to its mother nearby. *Left*: A male frigate bird puffs out his red throat, hoping to attract a mate.

GALÁPAGOS GARDENERS AND ECOSYSTEM ENGINEERS

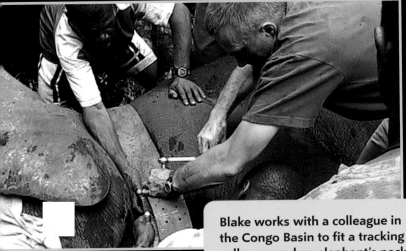

Blake works with a colleague in the Congo Basin to fit a tracking collar around an elephant's neck.

Before Stephen Blake began working with giant tortoises, he'd been studying elephants. It turns out that the two animals have a lot in common. Both are what ecologists call ecosystem engineers, and they have a big impact on the landscapes they inhabit. Elephants and giant tortoises are large animals that tend to trample and dig and stir things up. And both eat a lot of plants.

Giant tortoises are sometimes called the gardeners of the Galápagos because of their role in spreading seeds over the islands. Many of those seeds pass through tortoises' digestive tracts unharmed. They land in a pile of dung (good fertilizer!) and often sprout. Researchers have discovered that a single pile of tortoise dung can contain more than six thousand seeds from different species of plants. Sometimes those seeds end up nowhere near the plant they came from. Seeds can stay in a tortoise's system for up to a month, and a tortoise can travel a long way in that time, especially if it's migrating. Plants that sprout from those seeds provide food for countless other animals, in addition to the tortoises themselves.

Sea lions also play a part in the nutrient exchange between land and sea. After playing and feeding in the waves, they lounge on the beach by the hundreds. With plenty of food and no predators, these islands are a perfect place for them to live and reproduce.

The marine life of the Galápagos Islands is especially rich because it's a place where large ocean currents converge, or come together. This creates a mix of cold and warmer waters that's full of nutrients and perfect for marine life. The waters of the Galápagos Islands are teeming with dolphins, whales, sea turtles, and sharks, as well as more than four hundred species of fish that provide food for everything from frigate birds to sea lions.

Sea lions nap on the beaches of Santa Fe.

The Pacific seahorse is one of the world's largest seahorses and can grow to be over 1 foot long (31 cm).

A blue sea star clings to a rock off the coast of the Galápagos Islands.

Within this interconnected web of life are keystone species—organisms that hold the whole ecosystem together. Giant tortoises play such an important role in the Galápagos ecosystem that without them, other animals and plants would struggle to survive.

For many thousands of years, all that carefully balanced Galápagos wildlife was left alone and unbothered. People didn't even know the islands existed. That changed in 1535 when Tomás de Berlanga, the bishop of Panama, got lost on a long sea voyage and spotted an island. His ship had been blown off course and was low on supplies, so the crew stopped to look for food and water. They were amazed by what else they found. In a letter to the king of Spain,

Berlanga reported seeing "such big tortoises that each could carry a man on top of himself." Later, a Flemish mapmaker named the islands Insulae de los Galopegos, which means "Islands of the Tortoise."

Today, the tortoises that gave the Galápagos Islands their name are among the archipelago's most famous residents. Without their constant eating, bulldozing, and seed dispersal, the Galápagos wouldn't be the same. But these wrinkly faced giants almost didn't survive the arrival of humans on their islands.

CHAPTER 2

STRUGGLE FOR SURVIVAL

The story of the Galápagos giant tortoise is full of dramatic ups and downs. They arrived in the islands and flourished until humans showed up. Then their numbers plummeted. With the tortoises' survival in the balance, people came together in a desperate effort to save them. This chapter in the giant tortoises' history is still in progress, and what happens next depends on us. Saving the tortoises requires a clear understanding of where they came from and what they've already faced in their struggle to survive.

Once upon a time, giant tortoises walked on every continent except Antarctica. Most of those species went extinct during the Pleistocene era, sometime between 1.8 million and 10,000 years ago. Today, giant tortoises are endangered and live in just two places on Earth—Aldabra Atoll in the Indian Ocean and the Galápagos Islands.

Like other Galápagos reptiles, the first giant tortoises are believed to have arrived between two and three million years ago. Scientists' best guess is that several tortoises—or maybe just one gravid, or pregnant, female—were washed out to sea in a flood and rode the currents all those miles.

Researchers questioned that theory for a long time. Could a giant tortoise really swim all that way? In 1923 American naturalist William Beebe was exploring the islands and decided to try an experiment. He brought a giant tortoise from one of the islands onto his yacht and tossed it over the side to see what would happen. He discovered that while tortoises might not be great swimmers, they're excellent floaters. And because they can go more than six months without food or water, they'd be able to survive long enough to float that far.

Once the first tortoises arrived, they found plants to eat and began to reproduce. The islands turned out to be an excellent habitat, and with no natural predators, the tortoises' numbers grew and grew. Scientists believe there were hundreds of thousands of giant tortoises roaming the Galápagos Islands before humans showed up.

When more people arrived in the Galápagos Islands, life for giant tortoises changed quickly. Sailors, whalers, and buccaneers who visited the islands starting in the late 1500s discovered that tortoises could be an excellent source of fresh meat on long journeys. They would load dozens of giant tortoises onto their ships and store them alive, upside down in the hold, for food. This went on for hundreds of years, continuing after Ecuador annexed, or took over, the Galápagos Islands in 1832. As many as two hundred thousand tortoises may have left the islands on ships, destined to be made into soup for hungry sailors.

From a distance, giant tortoises resemble boulders in the fields and sometimes become resting places for egrets and other birds.

THE LIFE OF A GIANT TORTOISE

Male giant tortoises can grow to weigh more than 500 pounds (227 kg). Females tend to be smaller and weigh up to 300 pounds (136 kg). But all tortoises start out small, hatching from eggs the size of tennis balls. A giant tortoise takes about twenty years to reach maturity. Then it can begin to mate and reproduce.

A tortoise's sex is determined by the temperature at which its egg is incubated. Eggs that develop at hotter temperatures produce female hatchlings, while cooler temperatures tend to produce male tortoises. This also occurs in some other reptiles, including alligators and most turtles and lizards.

Giant tortoises spend most of their time—around sixteen hours a day—resting. (Wouldn't you if you had to carry around a 50-pound [23 kg] shell all day?) When they're not relaxing in the mud, they're usually eating. Giant tortoises eat a wide range of plants, including grasses, leaves, fruits, and cactus pads. They drink water when it's available and store it for a long time, so they can survive for months without fresh water.

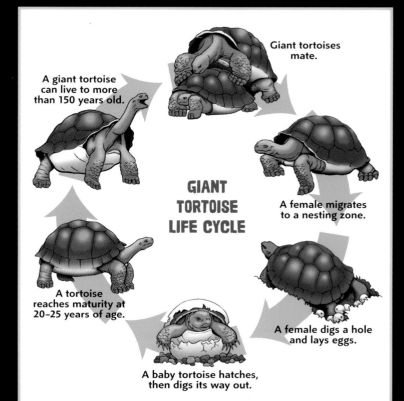

GIANT TORTOISE LIFE CYCLE

Giant tortoises mate.

A giant tortoise can live to more than 150 years old.

A female migrates to a nesting zone.

A tortoise reaches maturity at 20–25 years of age.

A female digs a hole and lays eggs.

A baby tortoise hatches, then digs its way out.

TORTOISE ANATOMY

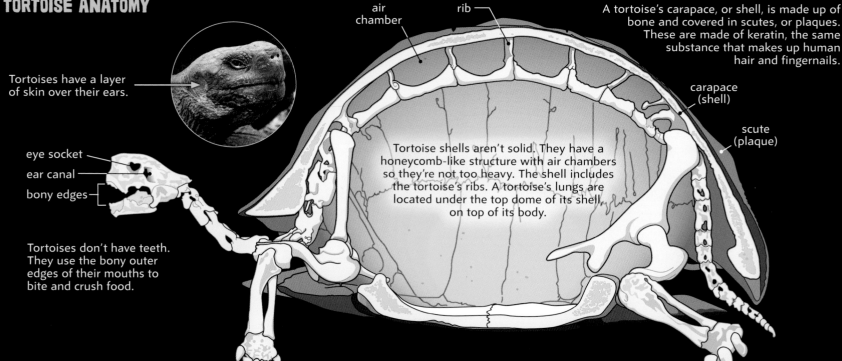

Tortoises have a layer of skin over their ears.

Tortoises don't have teeth. They use the bony outer edges of their mouths to bite and crush food.

eye socket
ear canal
bony edges

air chamber

rib

A tortoise's carapace, or shell, is made up of bone and covered in scutes, or plaques. These are made of keratin, the same substance that makes up human hair and fingernails.

carapace (shell)

scute (plaque)

Tortoise shells aren't solid. They have a honeycomb-like structure with air chambers so they're not too heavy. The shell includes the tortoise's ribs. A tortoise's lungs are located under the top dome of its shell, on top of its body.

The giant tortoise population was devastated. Scientists believe there were once at least fourteen species of giant tortoises living in the Galápagos. Today, no more than eleven or twelve species remain. No one is certain exactly how many tortoises there are, but researchers estimate it's between twenty thousand and twenty-six thousand—just a fraction of what the population used to be.

The tortoises' numbers were already in decline when Darwin visited the islands on his famous 1835 voyage, but he still saw them when he went ashore. According to Darwin's writings about the voyage, the tortoises seemed unimpressed with him.

Darwin also noticed that, like the finches, the tortoises seemed to have variations. "Several of the islands possess their own peculiar species of tortoise," he wrote. It's easy to see how those variations help tortoises survive on the particular islands where they live. On larger, higher islands where there's more rain and more vegetation, tortoises tend to have domed shells. But on dry islands, with less food available, tortoises tend to have saddleback shells that angle up in the front. That allows the tortoises to stretch their heads up higher to reach taller plants such as cacti.

"One was eating a piece of cactus, and as I approached it, it stared at me and slowly walked away; the other gave a deep hiss, and drew in its head. These huge reptiles, surrounded by the black lava, the leafless shrubs, and large cacti, seemed to my fancy like some antediluvian animals. The few dull-colored birds cared no more for me than they did for the great tortoises."

—Charles Darwin, *The Voyage of the* Beagle

Scan the QR code to see a video and hear what it sounds like! qrs.lernerbooks.com /hiss

What was that "deep hiss" that Darwin heard? When a tortoise pulls its head into its shell, it forces air out of its lungs and makes a noise that sounds like a cross between Darth Vader and a dragon—part hiss and part roar.

Those tortoises all came from the same ancestors, but they evolved, or changed, because they had inherited variations that helped them to survive in a particular habitat. This is another example of the theory of evolution through natural selection that Darwin would write about after his trip. He didn't talk about the tortoises in his famous book, but in the end, that book would help save them.

People realized how important Darwin's ideas about evolution were, and as time passed, the islands that inspired those ideas became famous too. Scientists flocked to the islands. Their stories of the amazing animals of Galápagos brought crowds of tourists who were eager to photograph the famous finches and tortoises. By the mid-1900s, it was clear that the wildlife that inspired Darwin's ideas was in danger.

In 1959, the one hundredth anniversary of Darwin's book, serious efforts began to protect wildlife in the Galápagos Islands. That year Ecuador passed an emergency law declaring that the 97 percent of the islands that was uninhabited would become a national park. That same year, scientists founded the Charles Darwin Foundation. The foundation's mission is "to provide knowledge and assistance through scientific research and complementary action to ensure the conservation of the environment and biodiversity in the Galápagos Archipelago."

The first job for the Galápagos National Park and Charles Darwin Foundation was to assess the remaining tortoise populations. Just how many giant tortoises were left? The news wasn't good. In addition to all of those years of mariners hauling tortoises onto their ships for food, scientists had started collecting them too. In the early 1900s, scientific expeditions from the United States and Britain arrived in the Galápagos Islands in search of specimens for museums.

On islands with wet highlands, tortoises tend to have domed shells (*top*), while on islands with dry lowlands, they have saddle-shaped shells (*bottom*) that make it easier for them to stretch their necks to reach vegetation.

In 1905 the California Academy of Sciences alone carried away 264 giant tortoises for its collection. As recently as 1960, some tourists who visited the Galápagos Islands took home giant tortoises to keep as pets.

By the time efforts to protect the tortoises were underway, just eleven or twelve species were left, most of them endangered. No tortoises remained on the island of Fernandina, where they'd gone extinct due to volcanic eruptions over the centuries. (Fernandina is the youngest of the Galápagos Islands and the most volcanically active.) People had hunted the tortoises to extinction on three other islands—Floreana, Santa Fe, and Pinta. Scientists at the Galápagos National Park and Charles Darwin Research Station realized that their work was urgent.

Soon after it was founded, the Charles Darwin Research Station set up a research station in Puerto Ayora on the island of Santa Cruz. Today it's the home base for the tortoise captive breeding program as well as lots of other scientific work.

In 1965 the Charles Darwin Foundation started a program to raise hatchlings in captivity. Now managed by the Galápagos National Park Service, the program helps tortoise hatchlings survive through the most vulnerable early stages of life until they can be safely released into the wild. One of the group's first projects focused on the population of Pinzón Island, where the remaining tortoises were old and in danger of dying out. New tortoises weren't taking the place of old ones because invasive rats kept eating all the eggs and hatchlings.

To interrupt that pattern, the scientists watched tortoises in the wild, waiting for females to lay eggs. Then they rushed in and collected the eggs before any rats could get to them. The scientists brought the eggs back to the breeding center, where they were incubated and protected. After the eggs hatched, researchers cared for the hatchlings and kept them safe from predators for three years. Once the tortoises were big enough to survive in the wild (and tough enough to fight off rats), they were brought back to their original islands and released.

Baby tortoises find shade under a rock formation at the Charles Darwin Research Station.

A sign at the Charles Darwin Research Station keeps count of the tortoises released on their islands of origin.

This captive breeding program also focused on Española, where the tortoises' situation was even more desperate. Invasive goats had made a mess of the tortoises' habitat, and by the late 1960s, there were only fourteen tortoises left on the whole island—twelve females and two males. Researchers knew they couldn't afford to lose even one more tortoise, so they rounded up those that remained and brought them to a breeding center on Santa Cruz. Then they brought in Diego, another male of the same species from the San Diego Zoo, to breed with the remaining females. Little by little, the tortoises began making a comeback. Those fourteen remaining tortoises (along with their friend from the zoo) ended up producing more than two thousand offspring!

Based on the successes with Pinzón and Española tortoises, the breeding program expanded to other islands. Since 1970 the program has raised and released more than five thousand tortoises at eleven sites in the Galápagos. Tortoises are doing well on the islands of Santa Cruz and Isabela, and populations are recovering on Española, Pinzón, San Cristóbal, and Santiago.

Researchers with the Galápagos National Park Service have also worked to restore land iguana populations, deal with invasive species, and manage the islands' growing tourism industry. They created the Galápagos Marine Reserve to protect the animals in the waters surrounding the islands. Park scientists also hope to learn more about the animals they're trying to save. They'd love to answer some of the many questions that Darwin wondered about when he first visited the islands.

One of those questions has to do with how tortoises migrate. When Darwin was in the Galápagos, he noticed that tortoise trails always seemed to lead up and down slopes, and he wondered why. Locals told him that it was because the tortoises migrated. They moved from the lowlands to the highlands in time for the June-to-November season of garúa, when the islands are mostly dry but a foggy mist hangs over the highlands. *Garúa* means "drizzle" in Spanish, and it's a perfect description of the weather in the highlands during this time of year.

Darwin may have been the first to write about giant tortoises migrating, but he wasn't the last to wonder about it. Galápagos park rangers have long talked about seeing the tortoises move from place to place based on the season, but there was no hard data about exactly when or how it happened.

Only stories. And questions. Why would a 500-pound (227 kg) animal choose to haul itself up a volcano every year? Was something about that slow, rugged journey essential to the survival of these magnificent creatures? And what other secrets were giant tortoises keeping about their lives and habits?

That's where Steve Blake and his team of researchers come into the picture.

The morning mist, or garúa, hangs over the Santa Cruz highlands.

CHAPTER 3

BABY GIANTS

Our tortoise-tracking mission in August 2019 begins in the highlands of Santa Cruz at a parking area for the El Chato Tortoise Reserve. My photographer and I pile out of Blake's pickup truck, excited to join him and Cabrera for their day's work. Gabriel Salas Sanchez, a certified naturalist guide, will come along today too. His presence is a requirement for our license to take commercial photographs in the park. There's a small walking trail at El Chato for tourists hoping to spot giant tortoises in the wild, but our hike will take us miles beyond that, all the way to the sea and the lowlands where the giant tortoises nest.

A fine mist drizzles down through the trees as we set out along the trail. August is known as the dry season in the Galápagos because the islands don't see much rainfall and the lower elevations dry out. But foggy mist still hangs over the highlands at the start of each day, so this part of the island remains green. That's why the tortoises migrate; they can find more food here where the dry season isn't quite so dry.

The big male tortoises, who require the most food, tend to migrate first. They've already made the long, rocky journey from the coast into the highlands. The females, who migrate a little later, are on their way now. They use the same trails we do, so we have to step around them as well as the boulders as we make our way along this rugged, rocky path toward the coast.

In the higher elevations, the trail is slick with red mud and littered with rotting fruit that's fallen from the trees. The sweet, tangy smell of guava hangs in the air. It's one of the tortoises' favorite foods, as shown by the many seeds that turn up in their dung.

As we continue toward the coast, the mud dries out and the terrain gets rockier. Cuban cedar and guava trees give

Above: The author and researchers hike along a trail that leads to the tortoises' nesting area.
Below: Poking tortoise dung apart with a stick reveals what a tortoise has been eating. This dung is full of guava seeds.

way to opuntia cacti and snarly, thorny shrubs. By the time we reach the nesting area, the air smells of salt water. Waves crash on the lava rocks that protect a nearby cove where flame-colored Sally Lightfoot crabs crawl over the rocks and blue herons stand in the shallows, waiting for prey. When we climb up the hill from the beach, we find a clearing where the earth is loose and sandy—just right for nesting.

A tortoise nest doesn't look like much—just an area of loose dirt. If you don't know what you're looking for, you could easily walk right over one. To protect eggs from predators such as pigs and goats, Galápagos National Park rangers cover the nests with wire mesh whenever they find them.

On average, only about one in five giant tortoise eggs will avoid the jaws of hungry predators and end up with just the right conditions—not too wet, too dry, too hot, or too cold—for a healthy hatchling to emerge. And once those baby tortoises venture out into the world, just one in five will survive their first year.

The odds aren't great for giant tortoises, but Blake and Cabrera are hoping their work might help. They're tracking twenty-five hatchlings, using radio and GPS transmitters to learn all they can about how tortoises live, what they eat, how they move, and how human activity might be affecting their ability to survive and reproduce.

Today, the tortoise team is focused on finding some of its radio-tagged tortoises. After checking in on five-year-old Angel, we set out in search of Paulo. Angel was fairly easy to spot, but Paulo is just a year old, so he's smaller and harder to find. Cabrera holds an antenna high over his head and looks down at the beeping receiver in his other hand. As he turns, the sound grows louder, indicating that the tiny tortoise is somewhere in that direction, and not too far away.

But where is he? Cabrera climbs along a ledge. The beeping is the loudest it's been, so Paulo should be right here. Is he hiding in the rocks?

Giant tortoise nests are covered in mesh to protect them from predators.

Scan the QR code to see a video of Cabrera tracking Paulo. qrs.lernerbooks.com /tracking

Researcher Freddy Cabrera searches for the signal of a radio-tagged giant tortoise.

Blake wriggles into a crevice holding a headlamp in one hand. No Paulo there. Cabrera circles again, then squints into a tangle of brush and spots the little guy under a tree. He wasn't hiding in a crevice after all. He was right in front of us the whole time, looking just like one of the many rocks scattered around him.

Cabrera reaches through the branches and picks up Paulo, who pulls his head into his shell. Cabrera places the young tortoise on a portable scale to see how much he's grown. He uses calipers to measure the hatchling, records the data in a waterproof notebook, and gently puts Paulo back where he was.

Paulo has grown since researchers last weighed him.

HATCHLING SURVIVAL

Tortoise eggs and hatchlings face all kinds of threats—from wild pigs, dogs, and goats to fire ants and floods. Some hatchlings die simply trying to get out of their nests.

When female tortoises lay eggs, they use their back legs to scoop soil on top of them. They mix in some of their own urine and dung, which later rots and creates heat to help the eggs incubate. "Once they finish," Blake says, "they tamp it down and piddle on top and tamp it down a bit more with their back legs to make this crust, which is probably an anti-predator strategy."

But sometimes that crust is too hard for the baby tortoises to get through. Because baby tortoises can die trying to get out of their nests, the Galápagos National Park requires that the tortoise research team lend some help to hatchlings in the nests they monitor. The team knows generally when hatchlings should be emerging from their eggs, so around that time, Cabrera hikes out and uses a machete to carefully remove that hard crust. Once the nest is open, he collects the hatchlings in a bag so they don't wander off. He weighs and measures them and then chooses a few to tag. When that's done, he releases all the hatchlings. They take off right away and usually move 200 to 600 yards (183 to 549 m) within the month, until they find an area they like. That's where they hang out eating and growing, usually for years, until it's time to start migrating. Cabrera just gives them a little help to get their lives started. Without it, the team would likely be recording even higher mortality rates.

We set off again, following the antenna and beeping receiver. Next, we find a seven-year-old hatchling named Samuel feeding on some native plants. The team gathers data, takes notes, and snaps a few photographs.

Samuel doesn't migrate yet—he's spent all of his time so far in an area about the size of a swimming pool, not far from the nest where he was born. But if he survives, in another twelve or fifteen years, Samuel will likely set off into the highlands as the dry season arrives. Scientists aren't sure how he'll know where to go, or when he'll decide to leave. The mystery fascinates them.

"One day, he'll say I'm big enough," Blake says. "I'm 80 or 90 kilos [about 176 to 198 pounds]. It's worthwhile for me to migrate up there. We can only hope that with our project we can influence land use so his journey won't be wasted."

Influencing land use means trying to keep migration paths free from fencing and other barriers that might block the tortoises' way. When Blake's team hikes into the field, they're not only checking in on tortoises. They're also monitoring conditions along the migration route. As we hike back up from the nesting areas, the team stops at a weather station they made in a clearing. Cabrera checks the rain gauge and records that just 1.2 inches (3 cm) fell in that spot in July.

Not far from the rain gauge, he squats down near a log and starts digging in the loose dirt with his hands and a stick. Before long he's unearthed a small electronic device about the size of a quarter. It's called an iButton, and Cabrera had buried it there to record temperature data every four hours. It was placed at about the

Left: Giant tortoises eat a wide variety of both native and invasive plants as they grow. *Below*: The tortoise team photographs their research subjects to help document their lives.

Cabrera collects data from a rain guage in the field.

Blake (*left*) and Cabrera download data from an iButton, a recording device that allows researchers to collect temperature data around nesting sites.

same level where tortoise eggs would be found in a nest, giving researchers an idea of what area nest conditions have been like.

As Blake downloads the iButton data to his field laptop, Galápagos mockingbirds flit from branch to branch overhead, as if they're part of the team too. This is one of fifteen weather stations up and down the migration route on Santa Cruz. "In order to understand why migration occurs and how it occurs," Blake explains, "we need to collect data on environmental variables that might influence the migration."

The rainfall data the team collects can tell scientists a lot about food availability. Temperature data offers clues as to whether a new generation of hatchlings might have more males or females. But in the end, it's the tortoises themselves that offer researchers the most information. Scientists say every bit of data they gather brings them closer

to learning the secret stories of these gentle old giants. And they never pass up an opportunity to learn more.

As we walk back to the parking area, Blake stops to look more closely at a small tortoise resting along the trail. The tortoise appears to have some kind of fungal infection on his shell that's causing some of the scutes, or plates, on his carapace to lift up. "It takes a lot of energy to fight a disease like that," Blake says. He pulls a small infrared camera from his pack and fits it into the jack of his iPhone. When he points the thermal imaging camera at the tortoise, his phone screen lights up with a red-and-orange tortoise-shaped blob that tells its temperature.

Blake also uses the infrared attachment to learn more about temperature maintenance in healthy tortoises. Bigger tortoises soak up heat more quickly, so they need shelter and shade from the sun, while smaller animals need shelter at night to keep their body temperatures from dropping too much. Galápagos tortoises also tend to warm up after they've eaten a lot of food and can lower their body temperatures to conserve energy when there's less food available. "That helps us understand the mechanics of the migration," Blake says. It offers some clues as to why a tortoise might choose to migrate to a different part of the island, where conditions are better for a tortoise of that size at that time of year.

But every time the research provides a bit of an answer, it also opens up a whole new set of unknowns. Blake and his team are now a decade into their research. Every day, they have more questions.

Above: A fungal infection has caused some of the scutes on this young tortoise's shell to lift.
Below: An infrared camera attachment for Blake's smartphone allows him to collect temperature data.

Blake stops to check on a tortoise whose shell looks unhealthy.

FREDDY CABRERA AND PROJECT ISABELA

It's easy to understand why Freddy Cabrera is so good at his job. His fascination with tortoises started when he was a kid, spending time with the tortoises that lived near his house. "It was the first thing I liked," he recalls. "I always wanted to be next to the tortoises." That hasn't changed much. Sometimes, he'll go out to visit his hatchlings even if he's not working. Cabrera likes to joke that he has twenty-seven children—a son, a daughter, and twenty-five tortoise babies.

He has a father's protective instinct for the hatchlings too. Cabrera was part of a project to get rid of goats that were threatening to devastate Galápagos tortoise populations. The goats had been introduced to the island by those same sailors and whalers who were taking all the tortoises. The goats reproduced and spread until there were more than one hundred thousand on the island of Isabela alone. Those goats ate a lot, competing with tortoises for food. The Charles Darwin Foundation and Galápagos National Park realized that the situation was urgent. If the goats kept multiplying, the tortoises might not survive.

Enter Project Isabela—a $25-million plan to bring in sharpshooters to kill all the goats, one by one. Cabrera led the project for seven years, racing over lava fields with his hunting dog and spending nights out in the cold. Sometimes, he'd chase goats up and down the same volcano five times a day.

When hunters on the ground couldn't find any more goats, the team sent up helicopters with sharpshooters to shoot them from the sky. And when a few smart goats eluded even those hunters, the team brought in a secret weapon: more goats. This group of goats had been neutered, so they couldn't reproduce. The team put radio collars on the new goats and set them free. Goats are social animals; they like to hang out with other goats. So the newly introduced goats eventually led hunters to those that were still hiding out.

Project Isabela lasted seven years—from 1999 to 2006. When it was over, all of Isabela's 165,000 goats had been eradicated. Before long, native plants bounced back, and so did tortoise populations. Thanks to Cabrera and the rest of the Project Isabela team, the mission was a success.

Freddy Cabrera uses calipers to measure a tortoise hatchling.

Invasive goats on Isabela Island, shown in this photo from 1994, were competing with giant tortoises for food.

CHAPTER 4

TRACKING HERBERT

Our second day of tracking tortoises begins on the property of Pikaia Lodge, a luxury hotel perched on an extinct volcano in the Santa Cruz highlands. The tourists who pay more than a thousand dollars a night for rooms here come as much for the wildlife as for the infinity pool and plush bathrobes. Giant tortoises wander the property when they migrate to this part of the island. Today, we're searching for Herbert, a tortoise the team tagged in 2010, when it first started tracking adult tortoises.

When the research team first met Herbert, the giant tortoise was already full grown, so they don't know how old he might be now. There's no way to determine the age of an adult giant tortoise. What the team does know about Herbert is that he migrates between the highlands of this area, known as Cerro Mesa, and a lower elevation closer to the sea, called Cerro Fatal. The team has been tracking Herbert by GPS all those years, plotting data points on a map to create a history of where he's been.

The Galápagos Tortoise Movement Ecology Programme team uploads information to a database called Movebank, which stores movement data from hundreds of species of animals all over the world. It's hosted by the Max Planck Institute of Animal Behavior, and its goal is to make it easier for researchers to save and share their data. That helps scientists to build on one another's work.

Today's search for Herbert leads us down a grassy slope in the shadow of the lodge. We hike through the drizzle of the morning garúa, looking out over a valley cloaked in mist. We haven't gone far when Cabrera's radio antenna picks up his signal.

Beep . . . beep . . . beep . . .

Scan the QR code to hear about this site from researcher Stephen Blake. qrs.lernerbooks.com /steve

Pikaia Lodge sits atop an extinct volcano on the island of Santa Cruz. Giant tortoises share the property with its guests.

The author joins researchers on a tortoise-tracking mission near the lodge.

...entists with the Galápagos Tortoise Movement Ecology ...gramme began attaching GPS tags to giant tortoises on ... island of Santa Cruz in 2009. Then they waited and ...tched to see what would happen, hoping for a glimpse ...o the secret world of tortoise migration. Would the data ...nfirm those stories Darwin heard about the giant ...toises' seasonal migrations?

...Maria, the first tortoise to be fitted with a GPS tag, rarely ...ved more than 656 feet (200 m) in 2009. But in late ...10, she started walking in a direct line toward Cerro Fatal, ...owlands area where her species of tortoise is known to ...st. She was migrating!

...nother tortoise from the Cerro Fatal population, Helber, ...o got his GPS tag in 2009. Researchers had found him on ...arm in the highlands, gorging himself on guava. They ...tched his movements, and sure enough, in early May ...09, he migrated too.

...o did Jumbo, who was tagged in 2010. But Nigrita, the female who was tagged with him, didn't. She remained ... the lowlands as long as scientists were tracking her.

As scientists tracked their tagged tortoises, they learn... more about how the giant creatures move. On Santa Cr... where the terrain is rocky and rough, the tortoises lum... along at about 437 yards (400 m) a day, taking two or t... weeks to make the full 6.2- to 7.4-mile (10 to 12 km) migration. Data confirmed the theory that giant tortois... migrate into the highlands during the dry season and re... to the lowlands in the rainy season. The tortoises spend... few months feasting on the new growth and then, whe... things start to dry out again, the males head for the highlands once more. Most females stay in the lowlands a while longer to lay their eggs, and then they migrate too.

Movebank maps track the movement of tagged torto... on the island of Santa Cru... The pink tracks show whe... each tortoise has been.

Maria

Jumbo

Helber

Nigrita

Herbert isn't like the elusive hatchlings we tracked the day before. He's enormous and impossible to miss, parked in the middle of a patch of dry reeds he's flattened. Blake approaches with the GPS base station so he can download the data from Herbert's tag. He's moving slowly so as not to disturb the giant tortoise, but Herbert sees him and turns to check him out.

As soon as Blake is within range, the base station picks up the signal from Herbert's tag. These GPS tags put out a signal every twenty seconds, looking for the base station. If it's not nearby, nothing happens. But the base station is in range of Herbert's tag now, so it gets a ping and then sends a message back to say "I'm here! Send the data." The tag sends the data it's been collecting every hour since the last download—information about the tortoises' locations and activity.

"We basically get a window into the secret lives of giant tortoises," Blake says as he watches the data load.

How much a tortoise moves depends on the season. During a regular month, a giant tortoise might only move about 33 yards (30 m) in a day, but during the migration season, tortoises can travel hundreds of meters per day. It's not an easy trek on short, stubby legs, but as we hike through the drizzly rain, we can see why the highlands are a good place for tortoises this time of year. Everything feels lush and green, while in the arid lowlands, green vegetation is more difficult to find, and the mud has grown dry and caked.

So why do tortoises bother to migrate at all? Why not just stay in the highlands, where there's plenty of rain and food

Herbert will likely remain in the highlands until the rainy season begins in December.

Blake waits for data to download from Herbert's GPS unit.

Want to see where all the tagged tortoises have been? You can use Movebank just as the researchers do. Go to www.movebank.org and follow the directions to find data from the Galápagos Tortoise Movement Ecology Programme on the interactive map.

all year long? Researchers think it's because the type of food in the two habitats is different. Vegetation that grows in the highlands tends to be tougher, harder to digest, and less nutritious. The lowlands might not have plentiful food all year long, but when the rainy season comes, there's lush new growth that's abundant, tender, and irresistible to tortoises. And at the end of the rainy season, after tortoises have had time to feast on all that new growth, the temperature and soil in the lowlands are just right for nesting.

The reasons for migration make sense, but not for every tortoise. Large male tortoises need more food, so it's worth it for them to migrate to find it. Small tortoises require less food, so for years, they can find what they need all year round in the lowlands and don't bother to migrate. But at some point, usually when a tortoise is in its early twenties, the balance tips, and the journey makes sense. Researchers think there's an ecological equation at work, a sort of tortoise math that allows them to determine when it makes sense to spend the energy required to migrate. What's that magical calculation? It's a question Blake and his team would love to answer through their research.

It's not only young tortoises that skip the migration. Some females stay in the lowlands year round as well, and the research team is curious about that. What's better for the overall health of the tortoises? Scientists are trying to answer that question by studying both migrating and nonmigrating females. They're comparing the tortoises' size and reproductive health to see which are laying more eggs and having more babies. Early research has provided an answer: migrating females tend to be healthier.

"They've got better body mass, they're tougher, and they have a higher probability of having eggs," Blake says. "That suggests that a migratory strategy is a better strategy."

But that answer led the scientists to new questions. "Are migratory tortoises in better condition because they can migrate?" Blake asks. "The ones that don't migrate might be sick or might not be doing well or might not be getting enough food, so they can't migrate. Or do the ones that can migrate do so because they're in a physical condition where they can?"

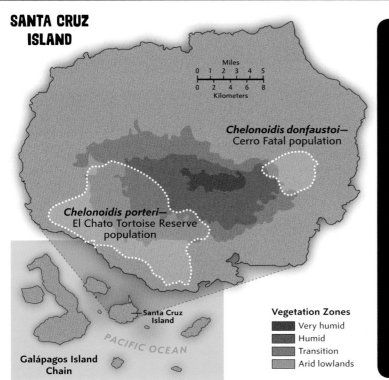

SANTA CRUZ
ISLAND

Miles
0 1 2 3 4 5
0 2 4 6 8
Kilometers

Chelonoidis donfaustoi—
Cerro Fatal population

Chelonoidis porteri—
El Chato Tortoise Reserve
population

Santa Cruz
Island

PACIFIC OCEAN

Galápagos Island
Chain

Vegetation Zones
Very humid
Humid
Transition
Arid lowlands

The research team is currently studying two different species of tortoises on Santa Cruz. An estimated six thousand tortoises of the *Chelonoidis porteri* population live in the El Chato Tortoise Reserve area and migrate up to 437 yards (400 m) in elevation. The tortoises that live around Cerro Fatal, a newly named species called *Chelonoidis donfaustoi*, make up a smaller population of about five hundred individuals that migrate between 55 and 492 yards (50 and 450 m) above sea level.

Female tortoises migrate later than males, partly because they're smaller and don't require as much food.

The research team is also hoping to predict how climate change might affect tortoises down the road, and migration is a big part of that picture. What happens if a shift in climate means that the highlands no longer offer abundant food?

The migration season of 2017 might have offered a glimpse of that uncertain future. That dry season, there was no garúa—no morning mist to provide moisture in the highlands. Plants died, animals couldn't graze, and farmers lost many of their cows because there wasn't enough food or water. It was bad news for migrating tortoises too. They'd spent the energy to travel all those miles, only to find that the usual feast wasn't there.

"Maybe under those circumstances, the non-migrators fare better," Blake says. It's one of the questions his team is exploring as they try to predict how future climates might influence tortoises. But coming up with those answers will require even more research.

CHANGES IN CLIMATE, CHANGES IN THE LANDSCAPE

Usually the giant tortoises' role as Galápagos gardeners is a positive one, as they spread seeds from native plants. But what happens when the seeds come from plants that could take over an island?

Researcher Diego Ellis Soto studied seed dispersal as part of his college thesis. "I had the pleasure of looking at a quarter of a million seeds on tortoise dung." He says the job wasn't as bad as it might sound, and he learned a lot about what tortoises eat and how they spread seeds.

"They eat introduced species in the agricultural lands and they disperse these seed cocktails into the Galápagos National Park," Soto says. Those "introduced species," or invasive species, can crowd out native plants. Global climate change means that the Galápagos Islands may be warmer and wetter in the future, making it easier for these invasive seeds to germinate—and easier for invasive plants to spread.

Invasive guava is a big part of the tortoises' diet. Soto and Blake counted guava seeds in tortoise dung at different elevations and mapped where guava trees were growing. Then they created a model to predict how guava might spread between now and 2070. Tortoises leave dung all along their migration route, from sea level to 400 feet (122 m) above it. Right now, guava only grows in the higher elevations, but that could change if warmer, wetter conditions due to climate change make lower elevations suitable. And thanks to the tortoises, the seeds will already be there, buried in piles of dung, waiting to sprout.

Guava trees are common on Santa Cruz, and tortoises devour the fallen fruit.

Diego Ellis Soto works with the tortoise research team on Santa Cruz.

CHAPTER 5

A NEW TORTOISE FOR THE TEAM

Day three of our tortoise-tracking mission brings us back to the Santa Cruz highlands, to Montemar, a misty hillside property owned by Roberto Plaza and Reyna Oleas. It's a farm, guesthouse, and tortoise habitat all in one—something the couple decided to build when they realized that Galápagos agriculture and tortoise ecology were sometimes in conflict.

"This whole project was born out of frustration," Oleas says, "because 97 percent of the Galápagos is protected and it may be in better shape than when Darwin came because of the efforts of conservation. . . . But [in] the 3 percent that's not protected and where people live, we're doing business as usual."

That business includes the agriculture that supports Santa Cruz farmers but can create barriers for tortoises. Galápagos farmers, who grow everything from coffee to avocados and papayas, sometimes build living fences called porotillo. These tightly spaced trees connected with barbed wire keep tortoises from eating their crops and trampling their plants. But the fences can also block tortoises from following their usual migration routes. In 2011 researchers noticed that Sebastian, one of their tagged tortoises who had migrated the previous year, had found his way into one of those fenced farms. He didn't migrate that year, and while scientists can't say for sure, they think he was probably stuck. Eventually, Sebastian found his way out and started migrating again, but his fence troubles make researchers wonder what might happen to migrating tortoises if more barriers are built.

Cabrera, who grew up farming in the highlands, says the problem is only getting worse as older farmers divide their land to pass it on to their children. "One father has three sons," Cabrera says, "and then those three sons inherit the land and it's this constant divide of property that's limiting these trails."

Misty weather in the Santa Cruz highlands keeps the vegetation green and lush.

Papayas grow outside the lodge at Montemar.

Cabrera and Blake hope the data they collect will convince Galápagos landowners to consider tortoise ecology when they make plans for farms and roads. It's hard enough for tortoises to migrate all that way through mud and sharp rocks on their slow, stubby legs. If more roads are built that interrupt their migration route, the trip will be even more difficult, if not impossible.

Plaza and Oleas hope their farm might serve as a model for other landowners to follow. They use a quarter of their land to grow coffee and keep the rest open as tortoise habitat. "We sell our coffee," Oleas says, "and with the money we receive from that, we're able to finance the rehabilitation of the farm." That includes working to get rid of invasive species that have pushed out native plants. Oleas and Plaza planned for the farm to be sustainable too. They produce all their own energy, harvest rainwater, and treat the sewage they and their guests produce. Houses on the property are made of mostly local materials, with the goal of reducing imports. "Because every time there's a boat or an airplane coming with things for Galápagos, there's a higher risk of introducing invasive species," Oleas says.

Plaza and Oleas have come to recognize and love the tortoises that use their land. One female in particular migrates up their way every year and likes to sleep near the house. "She's an incredible individual," Plaza says. "I think she's social. Whenever we go out of the house, she's sticking her head out to see." Once she even walked into their house when they'd left the door open.

"You probably built the house on her favorite spot," Blake says.

In addition to hosting migrating tortoises on their land (mostly outside!), Plaza and Oleas have donated GPS tags to help the research team with their mission. Today, the scientists are hoping to affix one of those tags to add a new tortoise to their study, but the weather isn't cooperating. The usual highlands drizzle has turned into a heavier rain that means any tag the team sticks on a tortoise right now is likely to fall right off.

Oleas pours coffee for the visiting researchers.

Left: Blake enters data on a field laptop
Below: Donated GPS tags are central to the tortoise team's tracking project.

GALÁPAGOS INVADERS

The Galápagos Islands are known for their endemic animals such as giant tortoises and marine iguanas, but as many as sixteen hundred invasive species also live in the islands. They include everything from pigs and goats to fire ants to introduced plants, such as blackberry and quinine. Some invasives are seriously harming native species, so researchers are constantly searching for solutions.

The smooth-billed ani (*left*) is believed to have been brought to the Galápagos by farmers who hoped it would eat invasive ticks that were harming cattle. The problem is, anis don't just eat ticks. They also eat finch nestlings, native lava lizards, and insects. Efforts are underway to manage this invasive bird.

Invasive rats are a threat because they eat tortoise eggs and hatchlings. Conservationists have set up traps (*left*) on some islands to help control rat numbers and save native species.

Philornis downsi, an invasive, parasitic fly (*left*), is currently threatening twenty different species of Galápagos birds, including the endangered mangrove finch. The flies lay their eggs in the finches' nests, where larvae hatch and feed on chicks, often killing them. Instead of letting eggs hatch in the wild, scientists now bring them to the Charles Darwin Research Station, where hatchlings can be hand-raised until they're big enough to be safe from the parasitic flies.

Fire ants (*above*) are believed to have arrived in the Galápagos Islands between 1910 and 1920. Tortoise researchers have found dead hatchlings covered in masses of ants. Efforts are underway to monitor fire ant populations and control them with insecticides in some areas, especially where tortoises nest.

The Australian cottony cushion scale insect (*above*) is a threat to eighty different species of native plants. Back in Australia, a little ladybug eats cottony cushion scale insects, so scientists in the Galápagos brought in ladybugs to help control the pests.

While the team is waiting for better weather, they work on programming the tags and getting everything ready. Blake sits at a table on a covered porch working on his field laptop and consulting with Cabrera to make sure the tags are all sending out signals.

A film crew from the UK has joined us for today's tagging mission, which makes the researchers' job a bit more challenging. It's not easy to work with half a dozen people around, maneuvering cameras and microphones on long sticks—but this, too, is part of the team's job. Working with film crews (and writers too) slows down the science, but it helps with education—another critical element of the project. The more people understand about giant tortoises, the more likely they are to support efforts to preserve their habitat.

By lunchtime, the rain has let up, so we set out into the fields to find the newest member of the tortoise team. He's a big male who pulls into his shell with that classic Darth Vader hissing roar as we approach. It's time to tag a tortoise.

1

First, researchers measure the tortoise and record data.

2

They prepare the shell by cleaning the spot and roughing it up with a file. This doesn't hurt the tortoise—it's like filing your fingernails—and it helps the GPS tag stick better.

3

After the filing, the spot is swabbed with alcohol to get rid of any residual grease. The tag will stick best to a clean, rough spot.

4

Researchers use regular epoxy from a hardware store to affix the GPS tags. It's the same stuff plumbers use in home repairs. Blake prepares the epoxy by mixing two parts together until it gets hot and puttylike.

The research team is hopeful that success stories like the farm at Montemar will inspire other farmers. But the issue isn't as simple as it might seem. And Blake is very aware that he's an outsider.

"In reality, we have all sorts of nice ideas," Blake says, "but I've never walked in the shoes of a Galápagos farmer who doesn't make enough [money] to send his kids to school. It's complicated."

Ideally, he says, tax incentives and other money would be available to help farmers preserve land for tortoises. But Ecuador's economy has been struggling for a long time. That money isn't there, so for now, the best option is more research, more education, and more conversations about how everyone can share these lands.

5

Then the team attaches the tag to the tortoise's shell, pressing it on and smoothing out the epoxy over and over. "You build a little ramp," Blake says, "so that when a tortoise is going through thick vegetation and hits a branch, it doesn't just bang against the tag but sort of goes over a little ramp, and you keep your fingers crossed. Hopefully it doesn't fall off."

Scan the QR code to see a video of this tortoise tagging. qrs.lernerbooks.com /tagging

6

Last but not least, the newest member of the tortoise team needs a name. The research team decides to call him Roberto, in honor of Plaza and his family's conservation work.

CHAPTER 6

FROM VOLCANO TO LABORATORY

Nearly 62 miles (100 km) from Herbert and Roberto's highlands home on Santa Cruz, scientists are monitoring another population of giant tortoises on Isabela Island. Unlike the Santa Cruz tortoises, these tortoises live in a remote, unpopulated area. The trip to visit them involves a bumpy, three-hour boat ride and a slippery beach landing, followed by a seven-hour hike up an active volcano called Alcedo. Researchers make the climb hauling all their supplies, including a portable generator and cooler to keep samples cold until they can get back to the lab.

Sharon Deem, Ainoa Nieto Claudin, and other members of the tortoise team made this journey to Alcedo in July 2018. They settled into a primitive base camp and prepared for a week of work, collecting samples and gathering data on Alcedo's tortoises. Deem and Nieto Claudin work for the Saint Louis Zoo, which joined the Galápagos Tortoise Movement Ecology Programme in 2013, the same year the project got a grant from the National Science Foundation. Their job is not just to track tortoises in the field but also to bring samples into the lab to monitor the overall health of the population.

The researchers give each tortoise a physical exam that includes checking measurements and weight. Does it have any obvious health issues? How does its carapace look? Then they swab the tortoise's mouth, eyes, and cloaca—the opening under the tail where it goes to the bathroom and where a female lays eggs.

Originally, scientists had tried to collect samples from the tortoises' noses. The tortoises hated that.

"They just became crazy because it was very uncomfortable for them," Nieto Claudin says. So they decided to try samples from the mouth instead. "You have to kind of open the mouth from the side because you don't want to hurt their beak, but

Deem collects blood from a giant tortoise on Alcedo.

once you get in there, you can really swab away." The work was tricky for the research team at first, but two hundred tortoises later, they've become experts.

Researchers hope to learn as much as possible about the tortoises they examine. What's their overall condition? How likely are they to reproduce so populations can grow? Are they infected with anything that might make them sick? And how much stress have they experienced lately?

To find out about that, scientists test tortoises for levels of a hormone called corticosterone, which helps scientists determine how much stress the giant creatures are under. In tortoises, that hormone is tied to energy regulation, immune reactions, and stress responses. It can impact everything from how the tortoises' immune systems work to how many offspring they can produce.

The team is also looking at the reproductive health of two kinds of tortoises: females who migrate and females who don't. The scientists rely on ultrasound technology, which uses vibrating sound waves to produce an image, to look at follicles and eggs inside the tortoises' bodies. That's how they monitor the reproductive health of female tortoises and make predictions about how many offspring they might have. With endangered species, every single organism is important.

The team is also studying infectious disease in tortoises on Santa Cruz, Isabela, and other islands. To do that, they look for pathogens, such as bacteria, viruses, and other microorganisms. Recently, researchers have focused on four main pathogens that affect tortoise health: adenoviruses, mycoplasma, herpesviruses, and ranavirus. Scientists have already analyzed samples from almost six hundred tortoises. Many tested positive for some pathogens. Santa Cruz tortoises live fairly close to people and farm animals, crossing roads and agricultural areas as they wander the highlands. But the Isabela tortoises are different. They live on a remote volcano, miles away from any development. Will they carry fewer pathogens? Will they be healthier as a result of their isolation?

The team gathers at the Charles Darwin Research Station lab on an August afternoon in 2019 to find out. Project

volunteer Irene Peña has been preparing the Alcedo swab samples, frozen since last summer, for analysis. Researchers will use DNA testing to find out if the Alcedo tortoises are carrying any of these four main pathogens.

A segment of DNA that carries the code for a particular trait is called a gene. Your genes are passed down from your parents and influence everything from your hair color to your eye color to how tall you might grow to be.

When scientists want to find out if certain organisms such as viruses or bacteria are present in a sample, they can do that by testing for their DNA. Thanks to earlier discoveries, researchers already know what certain genes from the pathogens in their studies look like. To find out if any of those known genes are present in their tortoise samples, they'll compare them to known samples to see if they match.

Once a sample has been taken from a tortoise, the first step in the analysis is to extract DNA and amplify, or make copies of, a certain sequence of genes. To do this, Peña uses a special machine called a thermal cycler, or PCR (polymerase chain reaction) machine. The team likes to call

Giant tortoises on Alcedo are more isolated than those on the island of Santa Cruz.

Deem processes samples from tortoises on Alcedo.

Peña works with a PCR machine in the lab.

Deem and Nieto Claudin study the bands of DNA on a prepared plate.

it their "magic box." It amplifies certain sections of the DNA until there's enough to analyze.

Then the researchers prepare a gel and complete a process that lets them compare the bands of DNA in their sample to the known sequence. Those patterns show up on a special plate that Peña has prepared for the team to view today. It includes patterns for the first fifteen tortoise swabs collected from Alcedo last year.

"It's still warm," Nieto Claudin says as she lifts the glass plate from the gel in which it's been developing. She places it onto a lit screen for viewing, and the team huddles around to see their long-awaited results.

"Uh-oh. . . ." Deem had been hoping for different results from these samples, since the Alcedo tortoises live in an uninhabited area. But it's looking like they, too, have the pathogen called adenovirus in their systems.

Deem and Nieto Claudin lean in to study the plate more closely. It can be tricky to read the fuzzy bands of DNA, and a second look shows that things aren't as bad as they

seem. Just a few of these fifteen samples seem to be testing positive for adenovirus. One is a clear match, and two more are suspicious. Those samples will be sent back to Nieto Claudin's university lab in Madrid for more detailed testing to confirm the specific gene. Then the team will have a better idea of what they're dealing with. It might be the same kind of adenovirus they found in the Santa Cruz tortoises, or it might be a different kind entirely.

Nieto Claudin explains that the presence of the virus isn't necessarily a big problem. "It doesn't mean the animal is sick or going to die," she says. "It just means the tortoise is sharing its body with a virus."

All animals, from tortoises to humans, share their bodies with trillions of tiny viruses and bacteria. Most of these are harmless, and some are even helpful. But others cause harm. That's why Nieto Claudin and Deem want to learn more about this adenovirus in the tortoise samples.

"It will be interesting to see whether this is a new virus that's evolved with the tortoise here or if it's a pathogen that's been introduced," Nieto Claudin says.

The research team has also launched a study to look at antibiotic resistance in bacteria found in tortoises. This can be an indicator of how pristine ecosystems like the Galápagos Islands can be affected by human activities, such as farming.

Just what is this resistance, and how does it happen? Antibiotics include a wide range of medicines used to treat diseases caused by bacteria. Antibiotics are used to treat infections in many kinds of animals, including humans. You may have taken this kind of medicine when your doctor prescribed it for an ear infection or strep throat. Antibiotics work well, but when they're overused or used incorrectly, they can create antibiotic resistant bacteria. These are bacteria that are tougher than normal and can't be killed by common antibiotics. Sometimes scientists call them superbugs. When a person or animal is infected with antibiotic resistant bacteria, the illness is more difficult, or even impossible, to treat.

How do some bacteria come to have this superpower? It has to do with the same genetic variations and natural selection that Darwin noticed in the finches and tortoises. all those years ago. Any time antibiotics are used, there may be some bacteria whose natural variations allow them to survive the treatment longer. If a prescribed course of antibiotics is not finished, the treatment might kill off all but the toughest bacteria. When those remaining bacteria reproduce, they pass along that gene for antibiotic resistance to their offspring. The result is a whole new generation of bacteria that can't be wiped out by antibiotics. And because antibiotics kill helpful as well as harmful bacteria, there's even more room for the new antibiotic resistant bacteria to multiply. Antibiotics that are disposed of improperly can lead to similar problems.

The same thing can happen when antibiotics are used too often, used without a doctor's guidance, or used for illnesses that aren't caused by bacteria. The more antibiotics are used, the more likely resistance will occur.

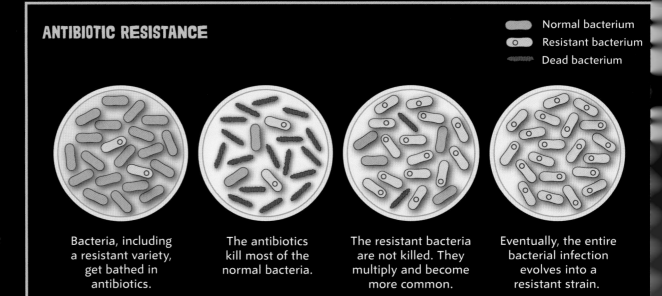

ANTIBIOTIC RESISTANCE

Normal bacterium
Resistant bacterium
Dead bacterium

Bacteria, including a resistant variety, get bathed in antibiotics.

The antibiotics kill most of the normal bacteria.

The resistant bacteria are not killed. They multiply and become more common.

Eventually, the entire bacterial infection evolves into a resistant strain.

Tortoise researchers want to know what kinds of antibiotic resistant bacteria are living in giant tortoises' digestive tracts. Remember that all animals have bacteria living in their bodies, so even if researchers do find antibiotic resistant bacteria, that doesn't mean the tortoises are sick. But it could indicate how human activity is affecting bacteria in the Galápagos ecosystem.

Nieto Claudin and Deem launched the study by analyzing fecal samples, or poop samples, from thirty Santa Cruz tortoises. They used DNA testing to find out if any samples contained genes that make bacteria resistant to eight different groups of common antibiotics. The results were alarming. Every single tortoise was carrying bacteria that was resistant to at least one family of commonly used antibiotic.

That could mean trouble not only for tortoises but for farm animals as well. Antibiotic resistant bacteria can cause serious diseases that are difficult to treat. When those bacteria become widespread, it can lead to huge losses of farm animals. The more antibiotics are used, the worse the problem is likely to become. Right now, Ecuador doesn't regulate most antibiotics; you can buy them at the drugstore without a prescription. The research team would like to see more regulation. They're sharing their findings, hoping to help people understand that the health of the Galápagos tortoises is linked to livestock and human health.

"Then you can get more people to care," Deem says. "If we show that this is actually a public health issue as well as a conservation challenge, we're hopeful that can help."

Scientists are teaching about a concept called One Health, the idea that human health, animal health, and the health of the environment are all connected. More people live on the planet, and they're spreading into areas that used to be

When tortoises migrate, they pass through farmlands and other areas where people live. It's not uncommon to see one crossing the road—or just sitting in the middle of it.

wild. As a result, people live in closer contact with wildlife, and this can lead to the spread of disease. Travel and transportation are easier and faster than ever. That's great for getting people and goods from place to place but also allows for the spread of disease. Fewer forests and warming global temperatures can also lead to public health problems.

Animals can serve as an early warning sign that humans are in danger. Some diseases, such as mosquito-borne illnesses like West Nile virus, affect both humans and other animals. A sudden appearance of dead birds can alert scientists that a human outbreak of West Nile virus may be on the way. Those early warnings help them monitor how the disease may be spreading due to changes in climate.

Environmental changes affect everything from the spread of disease to the availability of clean water, so it's impossible to talk about health without considering what a healthy environment looks like too. Deem and Nieto Claudin agree with other researchers around the globe who believe that a One Health approach—looking at the health of humans, animals, and the environment all together—is the best way to solve current conservation and public health challenges.

CHAPTER 7

TOMORROW'S TORTOISES

NO TOCAR
DO NOT

The Charles Darwin Research Station is crawling with baby tortoises—success stories from the captive breeding program. But the most famous tortoise here is a reminder of one of conservationists' failures. His name is Lonesome George. Before he died, he was the last of his kind. His species, *Chelonoidis abingdonii*, is now extinct. And his story is important.

Lonesome George lived on uninhabited Pinta Island, where for decades, scientists believed the last three tortoises had been collected for museum exhibits back in 1906. No one had seen one since. But in 1971, a biologist who was visiting the island spotted a tortoise and reported it. A few months later, park rangers found that lone tortoise and brought him to the research center on Santa Cruz.

There was great excitement. This species that was thought to be gone wasn't extinct after all! Scientists named the tortoise Lonesome George. In 1996 they put him in a pen with two female tortoises from a closely related species, hoping they might mate.

But years passed, and there were no babies. In 2008, there was a glimmer of hope when the females nested and laid eggs, but the eggs turned out to be infertile. They never hatched. And in 2012, Lonesome George, the last male Pinta Island tortoise, died. The National Park Service had his body taxidermied, or preserved, so that visitors could see him. The exhibit's story isn't a happy one, but it's an essential reminder of what's at stake. Scientists hope it will help build support for the work they're doing not far from George's exhibit.

Just down a dirt path from Lonesome George's building, the fenced enclosures are full of babies. Hatchlings of every age toddle around on sturdy little legs, growing and waiting for the day they can return to their natural habitats. If all goes well, they'll be climbing over rocks and munching on plants long after all their researchers are gone. That's something the tortoise scientists try to keep in mind as they trudge out into the field each day and sort samples by headlight into the night.

They're doing the short-term work every day, downloading data, writing papers, and sharing results, hoping people will consider tortoise ecology as they make laws and run farms. But they're also playing a long game. Even as they deal with the threats tortoises face today, they're trying to anticipate what might come next.

Tortoise hatchlings are raised in enclosures at the Charles Darwin Research Station.

Climate change tops their list of concerns. Studies have shown that warming global temperatures are already affecting the Galápagos Islands. Corals in the surrounding waters are bleaching—an early warning sign that more widespread impacts may be ahead. If the climate grows warmer and wetter, floods could wash away the trees where finches nest.

Iguanas might not be able to regulate their body temperatures as well. Sea lions and other animals might have to travel farther in search of food. And the changes might allow invasive species to spread even more quickly. Those parasitic fly larvae that have been devouring the finch eggs and chicks thrive in warm, wet conditions.

In 2011 Conservation International and the World Wildlife Fund did a study on which animals might be harmed by global warming. The groups reported that sea turtles, iguanas, Galápagos penguins, blue-footed boobies, and sea lions are all expected to drop in population. Giant tortoises are on that list too. Scientists are especially concerned about how a warmer, wetter climate might affect nesting.

"Rainfall is a blessing and a curse for the tortoises," Blake says. High rainfall means plenty of plants to eat. But too much rain can flood nests, causing tortoises to suffocate in their eggs. "There's a fine balance between how much rain is good and how much is too much." Blake is concerned that changing cycles of El Niño, a weather pattern that brings lots of rain, could result in more years when many small hatchlings drown, or even years when no eggs survive at all.

He's also wondering what will happen if warmer temperatures change the sex ratio of tortoises born in the wild. Don't forget that temperature determines the sex of developing tortoises. What happens if it's too hot for male tortoises to develop, and only females are born? It might

Iguanas and sea turtles are among the Galápagos animals that could be affected by global warming.

sound like an idea from a science fiction movie, but scientists are starting to see a shift in male-female numbers in sea turtles on the Great Barrier Reef and the Cabo Verde Islands.

This team of researchers can almost hear the clock ticking as they work. "We just now know enough to be asking the right questions," Blake says. The more answers his team can come up with, the better the chances they'll be able to help these gentle giants survive the changes coming their way.

"Can tortoises be flexible in where they nest?" Blake wonders. He hasn't been studying his tagged individuals long enough to know for sure if they return to nest in the same place they hatched, as many species of turtles do. "If there's no flexibility in where you can nest as a female, then you're at the mercy of climate completely." Blake estimates that if rainfall in the islands increases by 30 percent over the next twenty years, most current nesting sites won't be usable. What will the research team do then? Will giant tortoises have to be bred only in captivity?

The other change rushing headlong at the tortoise population is the Galápagos economy. Tourism in the islands has taken off in recent years. In 1950 only 1,000 people came to visit the islands. By 2018 that number had jumped to over 275,000. In some ways, that's helpful. Tourists bring money that helps to support not only the businesses of people who live in the islands but also conservation programs.

But the numbers are overwhelming. The UNESCO World Heritage Committee has put Galápagos on a list of endangered sites, due to that rush of tourism, combined with population growth, invasive species, and overfishing. UNESCO concluded that development and growth in the Galápagos Islands can't continue at its current rate if wildlife is going to survive.

Our naturalist guide, Gabriel Salas Sanchez, grew up with the giant tortoises, and he loves teaching local kids and visitors about them. But right now, he says, there are too many visitors to keep track of. He's seen tourists who weren't with a guide walk right up to tortoises on a farm and touch them, completely ignoring rules that require people to stay 6 feet (1.8 m) from wildlife. "It's not cool that somebody comes into your house and starts touching you," Sanchez says. He'd like to see limits on the number of people allowed to visit each year.

Friendly people, wildlife, and beautiful beaches draw tourists to the Galápagos Islands, but some worry that too many visitors are harming wildlife.

JOIN THE TORTOISE TEAM

If you and your family or class would like to be part of the tortoise team, they're always looking for support. You can visit https://www.stlzoo.org /conservation/institute-for-conservation-medicine to learn about the Saint Louis Zoo Institute for Conservation Medicine and make a donation.

Here's how your money can help:

A $50 donation provides daily transportation to the field for researchers to collect health samples from tortoises.

A $150 donation will pay for one VHF radio device to tag one baby tortoise.

A $1,500 donation can purchase one GPS tag to tag one adult tortoise or provide the monthly salary for a junior scientist with the team.

Donations help fund the tortoise researchers' work.

For now, scientists believe that more research and more education are their best tools for ensuring the tortoises' survival. Blake is in a curious position, studying creatures that are virtually guaranteed to outlive him. He's trying to secure longer-term funding for his team's research and hopes to find an Ecuadorian scientist to take over his role as head of the tortoise project. That way, ownership of the ecology efforts can rest with the people who live there and share the tortoises' home.

Education is an essential piece of the scientists' mission. The research team works not only with Galápagos officials but also with the islands' young people. Blake and Cabrera bring local kids into the field with them to meet the giant tortoises that visitors come so far to see. Deem and Nieto Claudin invite students into the lab, where they learn about scientific analysis. They look at tortoise blood samples under a microscope and use a special tool to count the different kinds of cells.

Cabrera prepares to tag a giant tortoise.

"For most, it's their first time using a microscope," Deem says. "That's a way they can practice and learn and play with the different tools of the lab and have the feeling of what it's like to be a scientist."

The tortoise researchers understand their work is a long way from finished. They're counting on a new generation of scientists to continue the research and conservation efforts, to make sure giant tortoises survive the challenges they face, today and into the future.

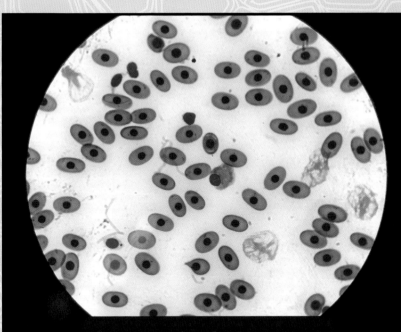

Scientists teach students to use a special counter to keep track of blood cells seen under a microscope.

Scan the QR code to see how researchers train student scientists to help in the lab. qrs.lernerbooks.com /training

Nieto Claudin studies a tortoise blood sample under the microscope.

AUTHOR'S NOTE

As a lifelong naturalist, I've always been fascinated with the unique wildlife of the Galápagos Islands. As a kid, I'd watch nature shows on television and read about the animals in my *World Book Encyclopedia*. I never imagined I'd have the opportunity to travel there and tag along with a team of scientists doing work that could save an endangered species.

But in August 2019, I peered out an airplane window as the islands came into view beneath the clouds. As soon as my family landed at the airport in Baltra, it was clear this was no ordinary place. It was like nowhere else on Earth and required special protection. Signs around the airport outlined the Galápagos Islands' conservation

policies, including a ban on plastic straws, bottles, bags, and Styrofoam containers.

Before our plane landed, flight attendants had walked through to spray insecticide into the overhead compartments, to make sure no invasive insects had stowed away in anyone's luggage. As we passed through the airport, officials searched our bags for anything that could damage the islands' fragile ecosystem. My mud-stained hiking boots warranted a closer look. "Where do you live?" an officer asked. When I explained that the boots and I had come from Upstate New York, he nodded and waved me through.

For the next week, my family and I came to understand what all of those safeguards are in place to protect. On the days my photographer son Jake and I weren't hiking through the brush or awaiting test results with researchers in the lab, my family spent time exploring the islands' rich land and marine life.

We visited the Charles Darwin Research Station and met its resident tortoises. We hiked the designated paths of uninhabited North Seymour, Santa Fe, and South Plaza Islands, coming face to wrinkly face with sunbathing iguanas. We snorkeled with sea turtles that seemed as ancient as the ocean itself and with sea lion pups that darted and dove through the shallows, nipping at one another and at our swim fins in play. We rock-hopped between bright red Sally Lightfoot crabs scuttling along the shoreline. We marveled at the birds—the boobies with their spectacularly blue feet; the frigate birds with their bright, puffed-up red throats; and the ever-present finches that had whispered their secrets in Darwin's ear all those years ago.

And then there were the tortoises—wise and old and covered in mud. Walking the rocky, brush-snarled path of their migration route left me in awe of these ancient creatures—and with even greater respect for the scientists working to save them. I'm most grateful to the Galápagos National Park and Charles Darwin Foundation for approving our research and photography request, and to research team members Stephen Blake, Freddy Cabrera, Sharon Deem, Ainoa Nieto Claudin, Diego Ellis Soto, and Irene Peña for welcoming us into their lab and their world. More thanks are due to naturalist guide Gabriel Salas Sanchez, who accompanied us on field expeditions, and to my friend and former student, Josue Chanduvi, who provided much-appreciated help completing the translation of interview quotes later on.

Part of me would love to return to these incredible islands one day, just for fun without research or other work to do. But another part understands a difficult truth—that even as a researcher working on an educational book, I am part of the problem. My flight to Ecuador added carbon to the atmosphere, which contributes to global climate change. Growing numbers of visitors like me have led to more development in the islands, more imported building materials that can lead to the spread of invasive species, and less open space for tortoises and other wildlife. So while I'm grateful I had the opportunity to visit and to share this story with you, I won't be taking that just-for-fun trip. My week in Galápagos was more than enough to understand what a unique and fragile place it is, and why it's worth protecting.

A GALÁPAGOS TORTOISE TIMELINE

3 to 2 million BCE Giant tortoises arrive in the Galápagos Islands, reproduce, and evolve.

Before 1535 It's possible that pre-Columbian people from modern-day Ecuador or Peru visit the islands during this time period. Researchers are analyzing pottery and other archaeological finds to learn more.

1535 Tomás de Berlanga, the bishop of Panama, gets lost on a voyage and lands in the Galápagos Islands.

1600–1700s Early mariners and buccaneers visit the islands and take giant tortoises for food.

1800–1900s More sailors, whalers, and fur sealers visit the islands, taking as many as two hundred thousand tortoises for food. Others are killed on-site so their oil can be collected and used for lamps in South America.

1835 Charles Darwin visits the Galápagos Islands on the HMS *Beagle*, a voyage that will later become famous when he writes about his theory of evolution.

1859 Darwin publishes *On the Origin of Species*, a book about natural selection and evolution that was inspired by his Galápagos travels.

1900s Introduced animals such as goats spread through the Galápagos Islands, threatening tortoise habitats.

1906 What are believed to be the last three giant tortoises on Pinta Island are removed and taken to a museum.

1959 On the one hundredth anniversary of the publication of Darwin's book, a major effort is launched to protect remaining wildlife in the Galápagos Islands. The Galápagos National Park and the Charles Darwin Foundation are established and begin a review of tortoise populations.

1969 With tortoise populations in critical danger, the Galápagos National Park and the Charles Darwin Foundation set up a captive-rearing program for tortoise hatchlings.

1970 Twenty tortoises are released on Pinzón Island to try to bring back the population.

1972 A male Pinta Island tortoise found alive in the wild is brought to the tortoise research center on Santa Cruz, where he's named Lonesome George.

1996 Researchers begin unsuccessful attempts to get Lonesome George to breed with female tortoises.

1999 Officials launch Project Isabela to eradicate invasive goats.

2006 Project Isabela is declared a success, as all invasive goats have been removed from Isabela.

2009 The Galápagos Tortoise Movement Ecology Programme is launched to study tortoise migration.

2012 Lonesome George dies without reproducing in captivity.

2013 The Saint Louis Zoo and National Science Foundation join efforts to study tortoise health with the Galápagos Tortoise Movement Ecology Programme.

2017 By the end of the year, more than seven thousand tortoises raised at the Charles Darwin Research Station have been returned to their islands or origin, adding to tortoise populations on Isabela, Española, Pinzón, San Cristóbal, Santiago, and Santa Cruz.

2020 The COVID-19 pandemic shuts down all field research in the Galápagos Islands, creating a three-month gap in the tortoise team's data. Tourism is also on hold, and many of the islands' thirty thousand residents lose their jobs as a result. Scientists return to the field in the summer of 2020, hoping to learn how wildlife has responded to this break in tourism and traffic.

GLOSSARY

antibiotics: a wide range of medicines that fight bacterial infections

archipelago: a group, or chain, of islands

biodiversity: the variety of life in a particular ecosystem

climate: the average daily weather over an extended period

deoxyribonucleic acid (DNA): the molecule that carries genetic instructions for living things

ecosystem: a community of living organisms interacting with their environment

endangered: in danger of becoming extinct

endemic: native to and living only in a certain place

eradicate: to eliminate, or get rid of

evolution: the process by which living things change over time as a result of inherited traits

extinct: no longer in existence as a species

gene: a segment of DNA that carries the code for a particular trait

GPS: global positioning system, a technology that uses satellites to provide a user's geographic location

habitat: the natural home of a living organism

hormone: chemical messengers produced by living things to regulate body functions and behavior

incubate: to bring eggs to a certain temperature so they develop

invasive species: non-native organisms that are introduced to an ecosystem, likely causing harm

keystone species: a species that other species depend on within an ecosystem

migration: the seasonal movement of animals from one area to another

natural selection: the process by which organisms that are best suited to their environment tend to survive and produce more offspring

organism: any living thing, such as plants, animals, and single-celled organisms

pathogen: a microorganism that can cause disease

predator: an animal that kills and eats other animals

trait: a characteristic influenced by an organism's genes

SOURCE NOTES

The primary narrative of this book is based on my field visits and interviews with Stephen Blake, Freddy Cabrera, Sharon Deem, Ainoa Nieto Claudin, Irene Peña, Gabriel Salas Sanchez, and Diego Ellis Soto in the Galápagos Islands during the summer of 2019. We conducted Skype and email interviews as well, and unless otherwise noted, all quotes are from these interviews and field visits.

Additionally, I've made use of multiple reference works and papers published by other researchers and experts in the field of tortoise ecology and the Galápagos ecosystems, and these are cited in the bibliography.

17 De Berlanga, Fray Thomás. "A Letter to His Majesty, from Tomás de Berlanga, Describing His Voyage from Panamá to Puerto Viejo, and the Hardships He Encountered in His Navigation, April 26, 1535." Galapagos.to. Accessed January 23, 2019. http://www.galapagos.to/TEXTS/BERLANGA.HTM.

BIBLIOGRAPHY

Becker, Rachel A. "New Giant Tortoise Species Found on Galápagos Islands." *National Geographic*, October 21, 2015. https://galapagosconservation.org.uk/projects/galapagos-tortoise-movement-ecology-programme/.

Blake, Stephen. Skype interview with the author, January 22, 2019. Personal interview, August 5, 6, 7, 2019.

Blake, Stephen. "Slow Motion." *BBC Wildlife,* June 2013. http://www.gianttortoise.org/linked/bbc_wildjune2013_uncorrected_last_draft_blake.pdf.

Blake, Stephen, Anne Guezou, Sharon Deem, Charles B. Yackulic, and Freddy Cabrera. "The Dominance of Introduced Plant Species in the Diets of Migratory Galápagos Tortoises Increases with Elevation on a Human-Occupied Island." *Biotropica* 47, no. 2 (2015): 246–258.

Blake, Stephen, and Diego Ellis Soto. "Sowing Seeds in Galápagos." *Galapagos News*, Fall 2018. https://www.galapagos.org/wp-content/uploads/2018/12/Galapagos-News-Fall-2018-for-WEB.pdf.

Blake, Stephen, Charles B. Yackulic, Freddy Cabrera, Washington Tapia, James P. Gibbs, Franz Kummeth, and Martin Wikelski. "Vegetation Dynamics Drive Segregation by Body Size in Galápagos Tortoise Migrating across Altitudinal Gradients." *Journal of Animal Ecology*, November 21, 2012. http://www.gianttortoise.org/linked/blake_et_al_2012_galapagos_migration_paper_aje.pdf.

Blake, Stephen, Charles B. Yackulic, Martin Wikelski, Washington Tapia, James P. Gibbs, Sharon Deem, Freddy Villamar, and Freddy Cabrera. "Migration by Galápagos Giant Tortoises

Requires Landscape-Scale Conservation Efforts," 144–150. In *Galápagos Report 2013–2014*. GNPD, GCREG, CDF, and GC. Puerto Ayora, Galápagos, Ecuador. http://www.gianttortoise.org/linked/galapagosreport_2013-2014-20-blake-144-150.pdf.

Cabrera, Freddy. Personal interview with the author, August 6, 2019.

Cabrera, Freddy. "Tales of a Tortoise Tracker." *Galápagos Matters*, Spring/Summer 2013, 16–19.

Cooke, Sophia. "The Introduced Smooth-Billed Ani." Galápagos Conservation Trust, December 11, 2018. https://galapagosconservation.org.uk/the-introduced-smooth-billed-ani/.

Darwin, Charles. *The Voyage of the* Beagle: *Journal of Researches into the Natural History and Geology of the Countries Visited during the Voyage of H.M.S.* Beagle *Round the World*. New York: Modern Library, 2001. First published 1909 by P. F. Collier (New York).

Deem, Sharon. Personal interview with the author, August 6, 2019.

De Roy, Tui. *Galápagos: Preserving Darwin's Legacy*. Auckland, NZ: Firefly Books, 2009.

"Galápagos, Lockdown, and the Impacts of COVID-19—Interview Series Part 1—Dr. Ainoa Nieto." Galápagos Conservation Trust, July 16, 2020. https://galapagosconservation.org.uk/galapagos-lockdown-and-the-impacts-of-covid-19-interview-series-part-1/.

"Galápagos Giant Tortoises." Galápagos Conservation Trust. Accessed October 9, 2019. https://galapagosconservation.org.uk/wildlife/galapagos-giant-tortoise/.

"Galápagos Tortoise." San Diego Zoo. Accessed October 9, 2019. https://animals.sandiegozoo.org/animals/galapagos-tortoise.

"Galápagos Tortoise Movement Ecology Program." Saint Louis Zoo. Accessed October 9, 2019. https://www.stlzoo.org/conservation/institute-for-conservation-medicine/galapagos-tortoise-movement-ecology-program.

Galápagos Tortoise Movement Ecology Programme. Accessed October 9, 2019. http://www.gianttortoise.org/.

"Galápagos Tortoise Movement Ecology Programme: Project Update 2016." Galápagos Tortoise Movement Ecology Programme. Accessed October 9, 2019. http://galapagosconservation.org.uk/wp-content/uploads/2016/10/GTMEP-report-for-website-Oct-2016.pdf.

"Giant Tortoise Movement Ecology." Galápagos Conservation Trust. Accessed October 9, 2019. https://galapagosconservation.org.uk/projects/galapagos-tortoise-movement-ecology-programme/.

"Giant Tortoise Restoration Initiative: Program Overview." Galápagos Conservancy. Accessed October 9, 2019. https://www.galapagos.org/conservation/our-work/tortoise-restoration/.

"Invasive Species." Galápagos Conservation Trust. Accessed August 14, 2019. https://galapagosconservation.org.uk/about-galapagos/conservation/invasive-species/.

Main, Douglas. "Galápagos Giant Tortoise Brought Back from Brink of Extinction." *Newsweek*, October 28, 2014. https://www.newsweek.com/galapagos-giant-tortoise-brought-back-brink-extinction-280593.

Nicholls, Henry. *The Galápagos: A Natural History*. New York: Basic Books, 2014.

Nieto, Ainoa. "Studying Galápagos Giant Tortoise Health on Alcedo Volcano." Galápagos Conservation Trust, October 25, 2018. https://galapagosconservation.org.uk/studying-galapagos-giant-tortoise-health-on-alcedo-volcano/.

Nieto Claudin, Ainoa. Personal interview with the author, August 6, 2019.

Peña, Irene. Personal interview with the author, August 6, 2019.

"Results from First-Ever Census of the Eastern Santa Cruz Tortoise." Galápagos Conservancy, December 1, 2018. https://www.galapagos org/newsroom/eastern-santa-cruz-tortoise-census-2018/.

Sadeghayobi, Elham, Stephen Blake, Martin Wikelski, James Gibbs, Roderick Mackie, and Freddy Cabrera. "Digest Retention Time in the Galápagos Tortoise (*Chelonoidis nigra*)." *Comparative Biochemistry and Physiology Part A*, 2011, 493–497. http://www.gianttortoise.org /linked/sedeghayobi_gut_retenion_time.pdf.

Sanchez, Gabriel Salas. Personal interview with the author, August 5, 2019.

Solomon, Christopher. "A Warming Planet Jolts the Iconic Creatures of the Galápagos." *National Geographic*, June 2017. https://www .nationalgeographic.com/magazine/2017/06/galapagos-climate -change-impacts-iconic-creatures/.

Soto, Diego Ellis. Personal interview with the author, August 7, 2019.

Stewart, Paul D. *Galápagos: The Islands That Changed the World*. New Haven, CT: Yale University Press, 2007.

Vela Fonseca, Joshua. "Seven Days at Alcedo Volcano." Charles Darwin Foundation, December 17, 2018. https://www.darwinfoundation.org /en/blog-articles/437-seven-days-at-alcedo-volcano-an-approach -to-the-galapagos-tortoise-movement-ecology-programme-through -photography.

Yackulic, Charles, Stephen Blake, and Guillaume Bastille-Rousseau. "Benefits of the Destinations, Not Costs of the Journeys, Shape Partial Migration Patterns." *Journal of Animal Ecology*, 2017. http://www .gianttortoise.org/linked/yackulic_et_al-2017-journal_of_animal_ ecology.pdf.

FURTHER READING

If you'd like to learn more about the Galápagos Islands and giant tortoises, you may want to explore the following books and websites:

Books

Castaldo, Nancy F. *Back from the Brink: Saving Animals from Extinction*. Boston: HMH Books, 2018.
Take a look at seven different endangered species, including giant tortoises, along with the scientists working to save them.

Chin, Jason. *Island: A Story of Galápagos*. New York: Roaring Brook, 2012.
Learn about the natural history of the Galápagos, including not only tortoises and other wildlife but also the volcanic islands themselves.

Collard, Sneed B., III. *One Iguana, Two Iguanas: A Story of Accident, Natural Selection, and Evolution*. Thomaston, ME: Tilbury House, 2018.
If you're fascinated by marine iguanas and evolution, this is the book for you. It takes a closer look at how these amazing animals came to be.

George, Jean Craighead. *Galápagos George*. New York: HarperCollins, 2014.
This picture book tells the story of Lonesome George, the last Pinta Island tortoise.

Heiligman, Deborah. *Charles and Emma: The Darwins' Leap of Faith*. New York: Henry Holt, 2009.
This biography for older readers tells the story of how Darwin's personal life, especially his relationship with his wife, Emma, affected his work.

Lasky, Kathryn. *One Beetle Too Many: The Extraordinary Adventures of Charles Darwin*. Cambridge, MA: Candlewick, 2009.
This picture book biography tells the story of Charles Darwin's life, from his childhood days collecting beetles to his contributions to science.

Websites

Charles Darwin Foundation
https://www.darwinfoundation.org/en/
The website has information about the foundation as well as links to articles about their research and conservation projects.

Galápagos Conservancy
https://www.galapagos.org/
The organization is dedicated to protecting the ecosystem of the Galápagos Islands. Read about the islands and wildlife as well as the organization's projects.

Galápagos Tortoise Movement Ecology Programme
http://www.gianttortoise.org/
Read more about the research team featured in this book and the tortoises they study.

Movebank
https://www.movebank.org/
At the Movebank website, hosted by the Max Planck Institute of Animal Behavior, you can view tracks for GPS-tagged giant tortoises as well as data from researchers studying other animals all over the world.

San Diego Zoo: Giant Tortoise
https://animals.sandiegozoo.org/animals/galapagos-tortoise
The zoo keeps giant tortoises and has a page with information about the creatures, including their habitat, diet, and family life.

INDEX

agriculture, 41
Aldabra Atoll, 19

Berlanga, Tomás de, 17
Blake, Stephen, 5–6, 8, 16, 25, 27, 28–32, 35, 37–39, 42, 44–45, 54–56
breeding center, 23–24, 53

Cabrera, Freddy, 5, 8, 27–31, 33, 35, 41–42, 44, 56
Charles Darwin Foundation, 8–9, 22–23, 33
Charles Darwin Research Station, 23–24, 43, 48, 53

Darwin, Charles, 14–15, 21–22, 25, 36, 41, 50, 59
Deem, Sharon, 8, 47–49, 51, 56–57
deoxyribonucleic acid (DNA), 13, 48–49, 51

Ecuador, 7, 19, 22, 45, 51
El Chato Tortoise Reserve, 27, 38
El Niño, 54
endemic species, 12, 15, 43
evolution, 11, 13–14, 15, 22, 49, 50

Galápagos giant tortoises
    anatomy, 20–21
    dung, 16, 29, 39
    ecology, 16–17, 41–42, 53, 56
    habitat, 7, 11, 21, 42, 44–45

health, 31–32, 38, 47–51
migration, 5, 7, 25, 27, 29, 30–32, 35–39, 41–42, 47
nests, 5, 27–31, 43, 55
origins, 12, 14, 19, 22
population, 21, 22–23, 33, 47, 55
reproduction, 20, 29, 38, 47–48, 54–55
Galápagos Islands, 5, 7, 11–17, 19, 21–25, 27, 32–33, 36, 39, 41–43, 47–49, 53–55
Galápagos Marine Reserve, 25
Galápagos National Park, 22–24, 28–29, 33, 39
Galápagos Tortoise Movement Ecology Programme, 5, 8–9, 35–37, 47
garúa, 25, 35, 39
GPS tags, 36–37, 42, 44–45, 56
Great Barrier Reef, 55
guava, 27, 36, 39

iguanas, 7, 12–15, 24, 43, 54
invasive species, 7, 24, 39, 42–43, 54–55
    fire ants, 29, 43
    goats, 24, 33
    rats, 23, 43

maps, 17, 35–37, 39
Montemar, 41, 45
Movebank, 35, 37

native plants, 30, 33, 39, 42–43
natural selection, 13–14, 22, 50
Nieto Claudin, Ainoa, 9, 47, 49, 51, 56–57

Oleas, Reyna, 41–42

Peña, Irene, 9, 48–49
plate tectonics, 11
Plaza, Roberto, 41–42, 45
Project Isabela, 33
protecting nests, 23, 28–29, 30–31, 33

radio transmitter, 6, 28, 33, 35
research, 6–7, 16, 19, 21–25, 29, 31–32, 35, 36, 38–39, 42–43, 44–45, 47–49, 50–51, 55–57

sailors, 19, 33
Sanchez, Gabriel Salas, 27, 55
sea lions, 12, 16, 54
sea turtles, 16, 54–55
Soto, Diego Ellis, 39

temperature, 20, 30–32, 38, 51, 54
tourism, 22–24, 27, 35, 55

volcanoes, 5–6, 11–12, 23, 25, 33, 35
    Alcedo, 47–49